What Would Angls Do?

Do?

How To Be Like The Archangels.

Crystal Dawn Doty

CI Publications, Inc.

www.clarityistheway.com

D1598709

ver art- Crystal Doty via Canva.com

nterior design by Crystal Doty

ISBN-13: 978-0692697276

For more, visit www.clarityistheway.com

or email angels@clarityistheway.com

I dedicate this book to my unstoppable warrior angels: Nathaniel & Nicholas.

And to my mother, who is my angel and believed in me until I believed in myself; who saved me until I could save myself.

I love you mom.

Watch Me Rise

You may have seen me fall and fail

I've been redirected, set a new sail

My new course to you may be a surprise

Watch me rise, watch me rise.

There is nothing I cannot do or be

When I know who is with me

No more will you see fear in my eyes

Watch me rise watch me rise.

I am the sun, and morning is now

"I Am the light," is my new vow

And able to see through the dark lies

Watch. Me. Rise.

-CDD

Table of Contents

November 11, 2015.

It was a dark night and a new moon. I could hear the breathing of my sleeping family throughout my house as I lay with eyes wide open like a child on Christmas Eve. My internal conversation weaved around several ideas that had seemed to be handed to me by something bigger than myself; this book was one of them. That night as I lay awake, I saw from the beginning to the end of what this book would be. I saw it in my imagination, heard it in my head, and felt it in my heart. I had always wanted to write a book, and I'd even started the obscure timeline of a novel. But never did I see this coming until that night. Never in my whole life had I been so excited to begin a project! When morning came, I sprang from my bed and began the process of delivering this manuscript to you.

Over the course of writing this book, my life has taken certain twists and turns as if situations and events were happening to inspire, encourage, and move me to write things I otherwise wouldn't have. The entire process has been a growing experience and many times ideas and concepts seemed to appear out of thin air and into the book, things I myself learned for the first time as I was typing! In all, this has been a peaceful and unfolding process, and an experience I hope you enjoy along with me as you read the pages that were written as if by angel magic.

For the duration of this book, I invite you to believe. I know life is tough, I know you have been hurt and roughed up, kicked around, and messed with. I know you had to grow up, and the burdens of responsibilities and obligations have covered your imagination, muted your bubbly laughter and domesticated your natural need and desire to be wild and fly freely. I know you've had to think logically and put away your secret dreams, and perhaps they are hidden from you now. Even still, I invite you to just believe. For a moment, remember what it was like when you were young and impressionable, eager to learn and grow and be bigger. Remember what it was to believe in miracles, and magic, and music, and how fun it was to dream and pretend. Remember what it's like to not be so serious, remember how to play. Right now, just choose to believe you can be anything, even a mighty winged warrior Archangel! I think that will make this book even more special to you. Anytime we choose to believe in the unseen- life becomes exciting again. Anytime we choose to believe, we choose to start living again. Read with an open heart, and watch the up rise of your soul.

Angel blessings,

-Crystal Dawn Doty

12-31-15

Introduction

When you think of angels you might picture sweet, rosy cheeked cherubs in renaissance paintings. You may also associate angels with religion, holidays, and funerals. Angels are depicted with fluffy wings, a halo, and seem to be without personality or much significance. It is as if their voices have been lost in old texts, legends, stories and myths. Because of this you may assume they don't exist, or that they have died off with the rest of the characters in religious lore or renaissance art. But what if they are more than what we have been taught? What if I told you that angels are here now and a big part of your everyday life? How would knowing that change you?

I know that when I first started to become aware of the angelic realm in the way I am about to describe to you, I began to feel very safe and secure in my life. I found myself with enough courage to take necessary risks towards my life purposes like the one to write books. I felt empowered, supported, guided, and I even started having more fun because angels have taught me how to lighten up. I realized that there is nothing I cannot do with these powerful beings by my side. They've given me strength in times I thought I would die; they have redirected me when I've veered into darkness. They have also shown me silent, tough love when it was time for me to rise with my own wings intact. And that is what I am here to teach you. Through my own experiences with working with angels, I have come to know them as the best examples of love, compassion, hard work, and commitment in my life. Whenever I have followed their example miracles have occurred.

Even though I'm talking about angels, this book isn't religious or even spiritual. You don't have to have any special intuitive gifts (although I believe everyone does) to connect to anything I'm writing about. You don't even have to believe in angels in order to receive really great ideas and wisdom from this book. This book is meant to be a grounded, practical guide for the modern world. Angels aren't ancient. They are here now, and like us they have evolved to appreciate technology and all of the modern day conveniences. They are very much involved in world affairs... to the degree they can be without hindering the free will of man.

And that's the thing; even with their amazing wisdom and power, there is only so much they can do. I see us living our lives thinking about how much we need help from Heaven when actually it's the other way around; Heaven needs us. So many people wait for things to improve, they wait for success to be given to them, they wait for peace to come, and they wait for love. However, the angels teach us that the solution to every problem is within us. Peace, love, clarity, and joy are within you and it is only when we offer these things to the world do we get to experience them. Yes, YOU have the power to bring what is seemingly missing to yourself, the people in your life, and every situation you find yourself in.

Anything that you feel is missing from your life is exactly what you are withholding from your life. This is because you think you are powerless.

You are not powerless. You have everything you need within you to correct yourself and the world around you. Most importantly you have a physical body and therefore the actual physical means to perform angelic actions. Angels need us to strap on our own mighty wings and be brave enough to do what they would do if they were in human form. Angels can give us the words, but we must be the voice of peace where that voice is needed. Angels can give us the strength to forgive, but we must be the ones who offer forgiveness to the world where it is needed. If you see anger, it is YOU who has the power to bring joy. If you see war, it is YOU who has the power to bring peace. We can recognize the discord in our world and in our lives, and we can pray to our Creator for help. But He will not send angels to our door to fix our problems, nor the problems of this world. He will teach us that all of our perceptions of discord are cries from this world and from ourselves for His love, and He will help us to find His love within ourselves so that we can then offer it to the world. Our Creator will guide us to take massive action to improve our own lives, so that we can be an example to others. He gives us His angels to guide us, not save us. His greatest gift to us is within our ability to perform miracles in our lives. We just don't understand who we are yet; we are only beginning to see that we are the ones who are to do the work and heal the world, and those of us who have figured out how are unstoppable.

Heaven needs us to be unstoppable, and to be our own heroes. We are the ones we are waiting for.

Times have changed. Have you ever wondered why our political leaders and modern day elections seem more like a bad reality show than a serious example of noble leadership? We wonder where the Truman or

Roosevelt of our time is. Our so-called leaders continue to astonish us, scare us, and let us down, and it's not necessarily because they are bad people. It's because they are not *supposed* to save us anymore. We are evolving out of that paradigm. There was a time when only a few people understood the concepts I'm about to present to you in this book- concepts and ideas of empowerment that were not widely spread, taught, or talked about. However, because this is the information age and humanity is developing, growing, and naturally becoming more self-aware and self-sufficient, we may not need the kind of leadership we have experienced in our past.

Perhaps, we are asking for more of a partnership with these leaders, as we can no longer follow them blindly. We know too much. Perhaps it will be "we the people" who end up making and enforcing positive changes. Perhaps it will be through our personal empowerment and betterment that will create the kind of society we all deserve to live in. Have you ever wondered why so many universities seem less attractive by asking students to go into debilitating debt for their education with no promise of a future? Especially now when so much education is available through books and the internet. Or have you noticed how more people than ever are leaving churches and organized religions in search for some sort of personal and unique relationship to themselves and God? We are in the process of questioning everything we've been taught and we are seeing a huge shift in where we are looking for leadership. Why is the self help section of the book store becoming as big, if not bigger than the business, religious, and education sections? As you look around at what we as a global community are doing, consider that it will not be your religion, your government, your university, a guru, or even your family that ultimately saves you. And if that isn't enough, we have a flood of global and economic drama that is currently providing us with the contrast needed in order to begin our own search; the search to find our true light, leadership, success, peace, and true happiness that we would not have sought out otherwise. In past times when we had great leaders and a booming economy, we didn't have to pay attention to our own sense of leadership. We didn't have to search for our true source of abundance, love, and energy. Whenever things are going great, we tend to not look for our inner desires and life's purpose because we don't have to. But when things are not so great, it forces us to us to search, learn, and grow.

The Evolutionary Turning Point

There was a time when men willingly aspired to work long hours for large companies in order to provide security, even if this meant putting his own purpose and passions aside. Women were content to stay home and cook, clean, and look after the children. Things ran smoothly and people at that time felt they had the American Dream. They were satisfied. There's nothing wrong with what we did back then, however we need to see how that paradigm no longer serves us currently. Through human evolution, it's not enough anymore.

Just like living as pioneers or pilgrims wouldn't work currently when at one time it did, what brought us happiness historically simply doesn't in our present times. Currently, people want community, authenticity, and equality more than ever. Evolving companies are becoming less impersonal, and showing a true concern, realness, visibility, and care for their employees. The businesses that stay stuck in our old pattern of treating their workers like machines will never survive this growth. This is one of the reasons our economy is so uncertain right now. The higher-ups cannot continue to do what they have always done if they wish to survive. They are losing power as more and more of their employees and workers realize there is more for themselves, more for our society, and more for the world than to be controlled through power and money. Economic uncertainty is one thing, but what I'm referring to is the actual price of life itself. The value we attribute to our time is higher than ever. We are seeing our own value- instead of waiting for something else to give us value. Standard job-for-life aspirations just don't do it for us anymore. More than ever, we are realizing our true life callings and we find more happiness in following our passions than staying in a "secure job."

I believe it's time to find ourselves within this evolutionary leap. No one else can find your happiness and passion but you, and angels are not only here to help you with that, they can be examples of how to fearlessly live your life's purpose. I believe it is time to save ourselves and this will require us to be extremely honest about how we feel about who we give our power to. It will require that we be brave enough to look within ourselves and take risks. And, as I will be discussing in this book, it will require that we focus diligently on 2 things:

1. **We must be willing to reevaluate our current mind state and habits.**
2. **We must be willing to do the necessary work and take massive action.**

Allow me to break these down for you.

Habits: A habit is a behavioral pattern that is created through repetitive thoughts that produce repetitive actions. Most people run their daily lives on habits that they either developed or were shown by family or society. As you read the following story, take a moment and think about some habits you partake in. Ask yourself if they hold any true purpose in your life or if you are just doing "what we've always done."

There once was a girl who was helping her mother prepare dinner for the family. Her mother instructed her to cut off the ends of a roast before putting it into a cooking pan. When the girl asked her mother why they cut off the ends of the roast, the mother stopped for a moment and then replied "I don't know, it's just what we've always done, it's the way I was taught. You might want to ask your grandmother." So the girl called her grandmother and asked her "Grandmother, why do we cut off the ends of the roast before cooking it?" Her grandmother replied "Well, I don't know why you do it, but I cut the ends off because it's too big for my cooking dish." The girl, seeing that her cooking dish was big enough to hold their roast decided then and there to cease the habit and stop wasting food.

If we evaluate the mother's mind state, she was only doing what she was taught and it made perfect sense to her until her child reevaluated the habit. Many times we have learned or formed habits that at one time served a purpose, however if we aren't willing to reevaluate we may very well continue wasting something whether it be our time, resources, money, or energy.

The Work: If changing your mind state determines what new habits you will create, then the work is simply the outcome or the physical actions that are taken due to the new mind state. Action must be taken. So often I see people focus on changing their thoughts, but their actions do not follow. To have a mind state shift without changing your actions creates tension in your life. You feel inauthentic and fake when you think one way and act another until your actions match your new thinking completely.

The work takes you from "being" something to "doing" something. The exact formula for a success in this area is:

1. Be.
2. Do.
3. Have.

This is a very important formula to remember as you read through this book. Many people do not fully understand what it means. They believe it goes in this order:

1. Have.
2. Be.
3. Do.

They believe that they need to *have* something first and then they will *be* someone who can then *do* what they want. For example, as this relates to money, many people believe they have to have money first, and then they'll be rich and prosperous, and then they will do all of the things rich people do. This isn't the way it works though. You must *BE*come rich and prosperous in your mind, develop an abundant mentality. Then with that mind state, *DO* what it takes to make that abundance a reality. Then and only then will you *HAVE* what you always dreamed of having. So, changing your mind state is only a part of the equation. It is the most important part. The next step is to do the work based on healthy habits that are inspired by your new mindset.

Here is another example of how powerful this formula is when used correctly. When the idea of dream boards (aka vision boards) hit the new age groups and self improvement industry, I was one of the many who hoped with all my might that by cutting pictures out of a magazine and visualizing those things in my hands, a big genie (called the Universe) would show up at my door and give me everything I wanted. I used visualization techniques and worked on my mental habits to feel deserving and worthy of the things on my dream board.

I love the idea of dream boards. However, I found myself stuck in the first step of the equation and my many dreams still unmanifested. I spent a long time in disappointment before I realized I was missing the next step. I was so busy reading, attending workshops, meditating, visualizing, and improving my mind state and BE-ing that I wasn't listening to the inner call to DO THE WORK and take action. I wanted to BE and then magically HAVE. This all may sound obvious to you, but I guarantee there are areas of your life you may be missing number 2 entirely without realizing it. You may be waiting for something to happen, or someone to rescue you. And that's okay; it's something that happens to the best of us. The work isn't easy, and most of us skip over anything that is challenging. However, once I realized the importance of action and began doing the work things finally fell into place!

The following is a story I loved as a child from Aesop's Fables called Hercules and The Wagoner. I believe it shows the general attitude of the Heavens when it comes to doing the work.

A Wagoner was once driving a heavy load along a very muddy way. At last he came to a part of the road where the wheels sank halfway into the mire, and the more the horses pulled, the deeper sank the wheels. So the Wagoner threw down his whip, and knelt down and prayed to Hercules the Strong. "O Hercules, help me in this my hour of distress," quoth he. But Hercules appeared to him and said, "Tut, man, don't sprawl there. Get up and put your shoulder to the wheel." And the moral of the fable is: The gods help those who help themselves.

We are here to attain strength, wisdom, and enlightenment. This requires that we constantly improve our minds, and allow our actions to represent the habits that lead us to success. It means that we have to be willing to change, improve, and evolve. And it means we have do the hard work. To me, no one understands this and can teach about this through example more than the angels.

I have found so much wisdom in studying the angels I write about in this book. They have the virtues we are here to learn, and they know how to guide our actions to benefit the entire world. This book will teach you how to improve your mind and your actions so that you can take the right steps towards your purpose and have the things you dream of!

"When you work you fulfill a part of earth's furthest dream, assigned to you when
that dream was born, And what is it to work with love?

It is to weave the cloth with threads drawn from your heart, even as if
your beloved
were to wear that cloth.
It is to build a house with affection, even as if your beloved were to dwell
in that
house.
It is to sow seeds with tenderness and reap the harvest with joy, even as if
your
beloved were to eat the fruit.
It is to charge all things you fashion with a breath of your own spirit.
Work is love made visible"

— Kahlil Gibran, The Prophet

By becoming better individuals, we better the world.

By studying the angels, we can gain a deeper insight in how to reevaluate our mind state and habits, and what changes we need to make in order to take massive action towards our dreams. As you make these changes, you may feel like you have joined a team of powerful beings who can lead you into your personal victories, and successes. The energy that gives the angels their power is the same energy within the core of every human being. You can absolutely be like the angels and do what they would do!

What angels are and what they are not.

Like I've said, it really doesn't matter what your beliefs about angels are in order to get amazing information from this book. But for a moment, let's all just pretend that we believe so that I can explain what I've come to know about them. Angels are not genies, as you have probably experienced through the disappointment of not having one show up with a box full of cash when you've prayed for it. They are not here to grant wishes. They are not short order cooks, matchmakers, or saviors.

Do they come when you call for them? Yes. Do they do what you tell them to do? Angels live to serve us, and they do everything in their power to help us to be happy. This is because they know that happy humans are empowered humans. However, if we ask for things that do not serve the greater good, and will upset our life lessons and purpose, they will often send us better ideas and inspirations and redirect us toward something better. So while you haven't won the lottery, perhaps you have a million dollar idea you're sitting on and you're too afraid to take action.

Angels are your companions, here to help you learn and grow. They are here to guide you as you fulfill your life purpose. They work tirelessly to orchestrate synchronistic events such as meeting your soul mate or being in the right place at the right time to receive a new job. They do not leave your side for one second, they comfort you when you're frustrated and they protect you from evil spirits and ill intentions of others. Your angels help you focus on your blessings- everything you do have, and help you to fulfill the areas you feel lacking in. They can help you understand why you go through what you must go through and help you discover your purpose and how to complete what you came here to accomplish. Basically, your angels do everything within their power- isn't it time we do everything in our power too?

The Guardians

Everyone has guardian angels. The way I understand it, we each have at least two. One who nudges and coaches you, the other who comforts you. Some people have more, and it all has to do with their life's purpose or if they've asked for more. Your guardian angels love you unconditionally, as they lack the human tendency to judge or feel offense. They are devoted to your life's purpose and by asking them to help, you open yourself up to greater assistance from the other side. They've watched you grow, and fall, and helped you get back up again. They are always there to lend a listening ear, a wing to cry on, a chest to pound on when you're angry, and they don't take it personally at all. They really are incredible. Isn't it amazing to think that we can be like them?

The 15

The 15 Archangels I am about to introduce you to are perhaps your strongest allies in this whole universe. My intention is to show you that they are not just faceless characters in the pages of old spiritual texts kept down in the basement of the Vatican. I want to bring them out of our childhood memories, and into your present circumstances. But most of all; the purpose of this book, I want to show you how amazing you can be when you decide to become like them. I want to bestow upon you the invitation to join the 15- the forces of light. The same invitation I received the night I was given the idea for this book. The one that is always open and waiting for you to accept. Whenever you're ready to be your own hero and make a massive impact on this world, they are ready to support you!

In the following sections, you will find alphabetically detailed information about the 15; their purpose, assignments, general demeanor, and their messages to the modern world. I will share with you how you can embody each Archangel and apply their strength, insight, and power into areas of your life. I highly suggest that you keep a journal with you to write down some of your thoughts and ideas while you're reading. If you're reading a hard copy of this book, feel free to highlight, make notes, and write in the book. Remember, this isn't just something to read to help you feel better, you are reading something that is here to help you take massive actions in your life; the kinds of actions these 15 Archangels would take if they were in your shoes.

Some things you may want to keep in mind as you read from this point:

The 15 will never treat you like a victim.

The 15 will expect you to find your power and take positive massive action when necessary.

The 15 are ready for you now.

Prepare to take flight!

Chapter 1

Archangel Ariel- The Activist

Take a Stand

She stands with strong arms open wide facing a beautiful sparkling pond. Her muscular legs are firm and her bare feet seem planted into the earth. With her eyes closed, she is breathing deep letting the wind blow through her wild hair. You wonder if the wind is coming from her or towards her, it's hard to tell. There is something wild, tribal, and beautiful about her. She lowers her arms and the wind stops. Somewhere off in the distance is the loud roar of a lion and this makes her lips turn up into a feral smile. Everything about her tells a story of unbridled passion and a strong care for the environment she now proudly looks upon. As you look closer into her face, you see the pride of a lioness. She is proud of nature, she is proud of her children, she is proud of her family. Although she seems unruly, unpredictable, and rough around the edges, there's a feeling that you could easily be accepted into her pride, and protected and fed like never before.

Archangel Ariel's name means "Lioness of God". Her purpose is to oversee nature and all of the creatures upon the earth. Archangel Ariel can help you with abundance, standing in your power, self worth, and giving and receiving acknowledgment. She reminds you to believe in yourself and that you deserve more. She helps you feel grateful for everything you have and to have a healthy pride in your surroundings. She wants you to feel your divine power because whenever you remember who you truly are, you feel serene and at peace.

She is the epitome of strength and fierceness. She urges you to take responsibility for your life so that you can stand on your own feet and be strong. True power is based on inner strength, self worth, and confidence.

Archangel Ariel is very concerned with the environment. It is her job to oversee how we interact with and treat nature. She is also very aware that much of the food we are buying is being tampered with, and this greatly affects us as humans whose bodies need fresh foods. The amount of chemicals we consume, and the way we are modifying our food is not understood by the 15, especially Ariel.

If she were human, she would be actively and fiercely taking a stand for the environment and other causes she felt passionate about. Being a powerful woman, she wouldn't just be on the sidelines with a picket sign. She'd probably become the CEO of a powerful company that would launch its own investigation to shut down the companies that tamper with our foods and the environment. She would be a fearless protector of animals, and you would see her trading her business suits for safari clothes to catch poachers and bring them to justice. Archangel Ariel, like a lioness, would be relentless when it came to the health of our planet. She would be on TV, radio, writing books, and doing what she could to educate people and expose those who seek to harm the planet. Anything she put her mind to, she would hunt it down and succeed. Because of her exotic beauty, strength, and the ability to articulate both common sense and deep wisdom, she would be an easy leader to follow. I believe in human form she would drastically change the way we are as a global culture and that her influence would change our relationship to the planet to be more like our ancestors- respectful, kind, balanced, and of service rather than of greed.

In her personal life, she would be fiercely protective of those she loved. She would see to it that her family received what they needed as far as material things go, and she would have an undeniable deep love and care for those in her life. You would feel safe in her presence. She would never come across as bitchy or mean, instead she would be powerful, fair and assertive. If she were to be challenged, you would not see her waiver from her beliefs and expectations. She would probably live in a big beautiful cabin in the mountains by a lake or river. She would enjoy hobbies such as bird watching, riding horses, and raising falcons and eagles. Much of her food would be grown herself, and she would enjoy gardening and preparing healthy meals. At the end of the day, you'd find Ariel bathing in a sea salt bath, resting after kicking butt at her cause all day. You'd see a satisfied look on her face, a glow in her eyes, and that smile... the one that appears after imagining a lion roar in the distance.

How You Can Be Like Archangel Ariel

There are obvious things you can do to be like Archangel Ariel such as cleaning up after yourself when in nature, supporting healthy local farming and honest markets. There's recycling and investing in products that don't harm the environment. But there's an even bigger picture to this Archangel. She is fiercely dedicated to her cause. She is unwavering in her beliefs. She is beyond committed to the betterment of the world. She has a healthy pride in her accomplishments and she loves to take care of those around her.

Archangel Ariel, like a lioness brings forth the idea of having a healthy pride in yourself and your accomplishments. What are you doing right now to make yourself proud? Are you working overtime for other people's approval? Do you have anyone in your life who is not giving you the approval you desire? If so, please realize that the only person's approval who matters is yours! Remind yourself that you are likable and lovable. Do not let others press your buttons. Stand tall and confident. Do things that YOU are proud of and see yourself, like Archangel Ariel, standing tall with security, strength, and a proud lioness heart!

When you accept all aspects of yourself, you feel centered and confidant. Then you can genuinely acknowledge others. If you want to be like Archangel Ariel, you must become aware of and nurture the good qualities of all the people in your life. People love and thrive on acknowledgment. It helps them to feel relaxed and secure in your presence, which is very much how you would feel in Ariel's presence. She is so sure of her power that there is no need to prove herself, and she is happy to shower you with praise and adoration. Her knowledge of her own inner strength is what gives her the ability to lift others up. She acknowledges herself, and therefore is able to easily acknowledge others.

If Archangel Ariel were a human, she would know how to financially take care of herself and therefore she would be able to take care of others. She would create income doing what fulfills her the most.

Being like Ariel means that you are willing to take a stand for your income too! What is your value and what are you worth? When you believe in yourself and trust that you deserve more, you will go after a higher paying career. Ariel knows that God wants nothing but the very best for each of us. He wants us to be open to receiving wealth and happiness. Of course, Archangel Ariel doesn't just work for the money; she also receives a sense of purpose, joy, value, and satisfaction. She gets to make a difference in the lives of those around her. She knows that the world is better because of her efforts, and her real paycheck is in the form of gratitude. Those things are the true riches of life.

Personally, I like that Archangel Ariel as a woman would be financially secure. Archangel Ariel represents capable, ambitious, take no-crap women who can provide for themselves in the context of finances and self worth. This leads to the confidence and safety in themselves when it comes to selecting a life partner. In what I have observed from my female friends, female clients and in my own personal life, I believe that women who are searching for a man should consider creating their own security first. This allows you to fall in love openly and honestly without any desperation or neediness. You are able to choose a man based on your absolute compatibility and connection rather than what he can buy you. I am not talking about equality or women's liberation, but simply the idea that the more secure a women is, the better of a mate she will choose. And men who find themselves with such a woman have the opportunity to offer her much more than mere dollars.

"If you don't stand for something, you'll fall for anything." Peter Marshall

The Mind State

Assertiveness: Your fearful beliefs about being bold can get in your way if you let them. There is a difference between being assertive and being pushy. Assertiveness comes from a healthy self esteem and either sets a healthy boundary or gets a point across while still honoring others feelings and beliefs. Assertive people are peaceful and fair. Being bold doesn't mean you are loud and boisterous; in fact many times your silence speaks louder than your words. Being upfront doesn't mean you have to be accusing or dismiss another person's opinion or push your beliefs onto another person. Being like Ariel means that you do not need to debate your beliefs with naysayers. After all, lions don't care for the opinions of sheep! Being bold means that you are very clear in your mind about what you believe and you are not afraid to express that belief with tact and in the right timing. Being a bold leader doesn't mean you make rash decisions based on hype, something to prove, or fear. It means that you take calculated risks and action based on the greater good of everyone involved.

Environmentalism: It may seem overwhelming to think about saving the whole planet, but if we each take accountability and responsibility for our own households, the planet won't need saving. Your example is far more effective than your rants. First, begin to be aware of the impact you have on your environment. Find one thing you can focus on to make your world a better place. Make one change to improve your environment, even if it seems small and stick to it. Second, Influence your circle of friends, family, and acquaintances through your example and watch the ripple take place. Every bucket of water had to start with a single drop! Decide that you are a single drop that will lead to an ocean of goodness.

Prosperity Consciousness: The quality of your thinking determines the quality of your life, if you improve the quality of your thinking, you will inevitably improve the quality of your life. Both poverty and riches are the result of a state of mind, and the most important single step you ever take on the road to wealth and financial independence is the decision to change your thinking. When you are practicing prosperity consciousness, you see life through optimism and a "glass half full" kind of perspective. You feel that there is enough abundance and prosperity for everyone, and therefore see no need for competing, rushing, pushing, and/or overselling anything. You believe in a steady stream of good things that consistently come your way, and you fully expect to see these good things in your daily life.

The opposite of prosperity consciousness is a lack mentality. This is when you see the lack of money and good things in your life, and focus on it until you feel broke, poor, and miserable. This thinking leads to actions that create self fulfilled prophecies. The desperate actions that are taken when you are in a lack mentality can be dangerous to your life and wellbeing. It can lead to cheating, stealing, lying, and working jobs you hate for the sake of pennies and dimes. No matter where you are in your life, you can at any time change your thinking from "there is never enough," to "there is plenty for everyone, including me." Right now, you can begin to look for the good in every situation. Recognize the valuable lesson in every setback or difficulty. You can choose to be positive and cheerful about everything that happens and you will be amazed at the difference it makes in your life!

The Work

Take a stand for the world. Is there something in the news, or some sort of public issue that drives you crazy? Perhaps those feelings are a sign that you are being called to serve a cause. Practice being bold in situations where it's less about you, and more about a movement you believe will bring greater peace to the world. What global, environmental, legal, or gender issue would you like to be a part of changing, and what steps can you take right now to make even a small one?

Take a stand in your own personal life. Right now, write down three instances where you may need to take a stand in your life. Just writing them down can lead you to start being honest with yourself. Whenever you are honest, you open opportunities for change that were not there before. For instance, if someone is treating you a certain way, you need to take a stand otherwise they will never have the opportunity to change their behavior. Decide right now that your feelings are more important than your fear of speaking up.

Take a stand for YOU. Sometimes you have to take a stand for what you want. Write down all the reasons why you want something and then put your foot down! Decide it's time to have it! At the end of the day, staying true to YOU is what is most important- you're who you have to live with every moment. You have to look yourself in the eyes, and if you're not being true to YOU, this will be hard to do. Go get that raise, start that business, say what you need to say, ask that person out, wear that outfit, start that new workout plan, buy that thing you want, write that post, just do it! Be like Archangel Ariel the lioness and go after it!

Real Life

A lot of the people I coach suffer from what I call negativity based depression. These are people who don't necessarily have a chemical imbalance as much as they are just seemingly born pessimists who struggle to see the sunny side of anything. Coaching them requires teaching ways to correct their habitual nay-saying and negative self talk. I find that a core issue is that they can become so engrossed in their misery, that it seems hard to see outside of themselves and their problems. Encouraging them to find an outside purpose where they feel useful and productive is very healing. I think it is a good idea for everyone to step outside of their repetitive thoughts and mundane lives to make a difference. It gives us a much needed break and helps us feel good when we can make a difference in someone else's life. One client in particular was working on his habitual negativity with me when I suggested he start getting outside more. "No, I can't stand all of the litter and garbage everyone leaves on the ground at parks and trails. It really ruins my entire experience."

"How do you feel about carrying a couple of garbage bags and cleaning it up on your way?" I asked with no expectation of his agreement. He paused. "Well, that's the only way I would be able to do it! These inconsiderate people obviously need a babysitter!" I told him to send me pictures of him on his walk, "babysitting."

A few weeks later I received a picture of him. He was standing with a group of people and they were holding up garbage bags near a beautiful river trail in the mountains. He was sporting the biggest smile I had ever seen. Attached was a message. "I think I've found my calling! And some friends! And I'm really happy right now! We are organizing trash walks and it's great." Then he proceeded to invite me to the next gathering.

Your happiness is in your calling. I am sure you've seen for yourself the joy that people can experience when they are making a difference. Perhaps service is an unstudied remedy for certain kinds of depression. As you align yourself to the powerful Archangel Ariel, you will see that taking action in service will not only empower your life, but it will empower those who are too afraid to put themselves out there and take a stand for their beliefs. So, reach out to the lonely, draw out the shy, advocate for those who feel isolated, poor, and hungry and comfort the sad. Your rewards will be a sense of inner pride, peace, strength, warmth, and love.

Archangel Ariel's Message To The Modern World: "*The world is an abundant place, filled with more wonder, food, and resources than you can imagine. However, it is the fearful lack-mentality that has you believe that Mother Nature cannot produce enough for you. Rest assured, just as* *a mother has milk for her baby, this planet has all that her children need when she is supported. When you see lack and limitation, recognize that it is only a reflection of what is going on inside of the human world today. The imbalance of power and economics shows in the imbalanced weather and terrain and there are extremes of feast or famine in this reflection. Your belief that there is not enough leads you to abuse the planet with chemicals and pollution as you attempt to hoard, change, or replicate what Mother Nature does. This is the age of information; the truth is loud and clear. If you believe that chemicals in your food do not harm you, or that tampering with Nature will get you more than simply caring for her, then you are closing your eyes and turning away from your Mother. The process of natural selection in these modern times will be a matter of who is making informed decisions and those who choose to ignore the evidence in front of them."*

Questions To Consider: In what areas of your life could you be fiercer? Are you able to look back on your accomplishments and be as proud as a lion? How can you carry that pride in your demeanor so that you exude strength and perseverance? In what areas of your life do you need to take a stand? What can you do today to improve the environment around you? Is there a particular world affair, cause, charity, or issue that really moves you? If so, is this something you feel compelled to become an active advocate for? These are some questions you can ponder if you want to be more like the fierce lioness, Archangel Ariel.

Chapter 2

Archangel Azrael- The Comforter

Love Never Dies

The rose was a soft shade of peach and he held it steady and obediently in his little hand. Everybody was watching, some with pity, some with despair, and perhaps there were a few who couldn't see him at all through their own tears. One small step after another, he looked down to see his new shiny black shoes make their way to the casket. He hadn't wanted to wear those shoes; they were hard and uncomfortable and this was the only day of his life he would have to wear such things. The shoes moved him forward, through the grownups, past people he knew and didn't know until he made his way to the center of the gathering. He could see the reflection of his flushed face in the shiny wood. It seemed as though his whole world was inside of that large casket, and all of the sudden it was just him. Everyone seemed to disappear and he ran his moist little fingers along the smooth edge. What was it like inside? He wondered what his daddy looked like under the thick lid, dressed in his finest suit, adorned with silk fabric and flowers. He looked down at the peach rose in his hand. He had just one thing to do. He had watched carefully as everyone else placed their flower on the casket but he felt so unsure. A part of him wanted to keep the rose, the other wanted it to stay with his daddy forever. But he knew the rose wouldn't keep its color- it would surely fade away along with everything else. Nothing felt real or solid anymore, why did things have to change? He finally set the rose softly next to the others on top of the casket. But his hand was only empty for a moment. Suddenly another hand- the familiar hand of his mother- was there to offer reassurance. He noticed her dress shoes as she led him from the crowd and he wondered if she was hurting as much as he was.

I feel it is no mistake that I am currently writing this section only one day after terrorists unleashed a dreadful attack on the city of Paris. I feel the planet still shaking after the horrific events that took place in the city of love and dreams. For me, watching the Eiffel Tower turn its lights off seemed to have cast darkness upon the whole world. So I lit candles. One for the city, and one for the world. In times of terror, the last thing we need is more darkness. Indeed, it is time to turn on the light.

This is how I feel Archangel Azrael interacts with the world. He is the first spark of warm candle light in the dark. You normally don't consider candles to make much of a difference until they are lit in the darkness. One simple candle can not only cast a powerful light, but unmistakable warmth as well. I often see Archangel Azrael as a huge enveloping candle light that is able to cover a single person, a nation, even the whole world if asked. He is like a warm blanket of comfort, and we are instantly calmed and centered in his presence. Last night, I saw him roll out his warm blanket of comfort over the city of Paris. I have no doubt that his presence was strong as he and his team of angels lead those lives that were taken into the light, and will continue to comfort those who are grieving. Tonight I pray that as the lights return to the tower, our hearts are relit with warmth as well.

Archangel Azrael's name means "Whom God helps". He is otherwise known as the angel of death. He helps us and our loved ones cross over into the light when it is time. He is quiet, comforting, and non-imposing. More than any other being in the universe, he understands grief, loss, and sorrow. It is his purpose to help us understand our own grief processes, and to maneuver through catastrophes and tragedies.

Grieving is an interesting thing. We rarely talk about it, and unless you have experienced a loss you probably don't know what to say or how to deal with a grieving person. I have found that in over 15 years of doing readings and life coaching that grief is the number one avoided process. We simply don't know how to grieve, and many times we instead do things to merely cover up the pain and numb the feelings. That is why we have Azrael. He is here to teach us to deal with grief, to walk us through it to the other side where we can find ourselves again.

If Archangel Azrael was human, he would most likely be a counselor, therapist, or someone who specialized in helping people through their death transition. Because he knows how important it is for us to continue feeling and communicating with our deceased loved ones he could be a medium- someone who relayed healing messages from the deceased to their grieving families.

Archangel Azrael understands that it isn't just death that creates mourning. We say goodbye to a lot of things in our lives. Perhaps a relationship has ended, or our children grow up and leave the nest. Moving, changing jobs, letting go of an addiction, a loved one contracts a debilitating illness or becomes disabled, being disappointed, a much-anticipated opportunity or life goal is suddenly closed. All these things and more can create a sense of loss- even if the change is for the good.

As a human, this angel would be the strong and silent type. He would rarely be noticeable until tragedy struck, then he would sweep suddenly into action using his gifts to help restore peace. He would most likely live in a city high rise, where he could look over the world. His flat would be clean, classy, and simple. Because he is such a deep being, I like to think that in his spare time he would also be an artist. It would be so amazing to see how he depicted renewal through pain in his art. Perhaps his art would feature in a gallery where it could touch those who were suffering.

Archangel Azrael would dress sensibly, in muted colors accented with pale yellow- the color of candle light. He would enjoy hanging out at the pub with like minded friends and celebrate the renewal of life. At the end of each day, he would light a candle and pray for those who are suffering before sending a caring text to someone who needed it. He would gaze out of his window and you would be able to see his vast compassion for the city lights below. Archangel Azrael would be a mystery to a lot of people, but deeply respected and cherished by those he helped.

How You Can Be Like Archangel Azrael

The world around us is constantly evolving, growing, transforming, shifting, birthing, and dying. In our own everyday lives, we tend to experience great amounts of pain when we find ourselves caught in the waves caused by these kinds of changes. Our suffering is not necessarily due to change, as much as it is to our attachments and need for things to stay the same. This kind of discomfort in the face of change is a universal experience, but since it is painful and uncomfortable to discuss openly the topic is often brushed under the rug. But treating our emotions of loss and grief as a taboo greatly hinders our ability to deal with them. It is necessary that we begin to talk about these emotions and how to handle change. Ironically, the one constant factor you can count on in life IS change, and there is no getting away from it. Accepting change as the norm allows us to be prepared, aware, and realistic. Being like Azrael means that when change happens; you accept it, even when it is hard. It means readjusting rather than resisting. It means no longer shying away from the unknown but fearlessly and honestly looking at the changes you must make.

Showing up for people who are in pain can be difficult, however I believe it deepens our self development and spiritual mastery. We often don't know what to say or how to help and so instead we do nothing, and leave those we love alone in the times when they need us the most. If you want to be like Azrael you are going to have to learn how to show up for people, even if it's just a quiet listening ear when they need you. There can be no more making excuses for why you can't be someone's comforting angel. Even if you feel like no one has been there for you in the past, break the cycle by letting it go and just start showing up. Don't be afraid to ask someone what they need. Bring them soup, buy them coffee, send them a text to let them know you're thinking of them, let them talk, hand them tissues, drop what you're doing and be at their side when they call for help. You don't have to have answers -- in fact it's best if you don't. They will find their own answers, but it will be easier with you there by their side.

Here are a few things I have learned from Archangel Azrael during my own times of sadness and in helping others grieve. For those of you who may be experiencing your own grief, I hope these tips will help you find peace.

1. Everyone will tell you to take care of yourself and you won't want to, but you must. If you are grieving over the death of a loved one, realize that they wouldn't want you to unnecessarily starve or suffer due to self neglect. If you are grieving over a life situation, you really owe it to yourself to be gentle and kind to yourself. If you have to, put alarms in your phone to eat, take

baths and showers, and get fresh air. Making sure that your basic needs are met is essential.

2. You cannot cry too much, or too little. Crying is different for everyone and there are no rules in dictating how much is appropriate for your level of grief. It is okay if you're a man or a woman: crying is not contingent upon your gender. It is a physiological response to painful emotions. You may cry at unexpected times or you may not feel like crying at all. It's all okay.

3. People might tell you that time will heal you. My experience is that you never really "get over" a deep loss. Your life will come back to you, yes. And you will learn how to navigate again and reenter the world, but depending on the situation your world may not ever be the same. You will have to learn how to live in it differently. Time will give you the opportunities you need to change and learn more about yourself through your process. Your grieving won't just fade out until you're back to "normal." You will have good days and bad days. Something might trigger a memory months or years later and emotions will rush back to you. Someone once told me that you never really stop grieving the death of anything; you just learn how to live with it and time will show you how.

4. Talk about it. Find someone who can sit with you, whether it is a professional, a friend, or a pet. You can even talk to your angels. Speak out loud, hear your own words. In addition to talking, write. Keep a journal of how you are feeling, and write down the things you might be too afraid to say. Write letters to the person you are missing. Write your future self letters. Address any regrets you have like things that were left unsaid or things you feel bad about. Be willing to be open and honest about your feelings with someone you can trust or in the privacy of your written thoughts.

5. Do what you feel like doing. Everyone handles grief in different ways, there really is no right or wrong way. Some people feel like they want to get right back into their routine, they want to work and carry on, and that is okay. Others may want to shy away from the world and lock their doors. That is okay too. You may feel like exercising one day, laying in bed the next. You may plan a trip and then decide against it. You may binge on junk food one night, or you may only want one type of soup for weeks. You may listen to the same song over and over, or you may just want silence. The

rollercoaster is real, and the only way it slows down is to ride it out. Honor your feelings, desires, and promptings. Your process is very unique and very personal.

6. Read books, listen to professionals, and don't hesitate to get counseling. Even though your grief is personal, it won't hurt to get therapy from a source that can enlighten you with experience and knowledge. Grieving is very much a time where we delve into our own personal issues, and having professional help can help you with your own self awareness and can even give you options and ideas you may not have considered when it comes to your healing. You can seek counseling even years after a loss if you feel compelled- there is no time limit.

7. Know when to ask for serious help. If you are worried about your grieving process and you feel like harming yourself, others, or if you are seriously neglecting yourself or others, please ask for help. Grief is already a debilitating thing to go through, don't add to it by doing things you will regret or feel guilty about later.

"The bitterest tears shed over graves are for words left unsaid and deeds left undone."-Harriet Beecher Stowe

The Mind State

Surrender & Acceptance: Acceptance doesn't mean we are necessarily 100% okay with things, it just means that we have surrendered our resistance to what is. When we are in resistance to what is, we are only looking at how horrible the situation is, and what "should" or "shouldn't" be happening. When we are in resistance to what is actually happening, we aren't looking to solve problems or to make necessary changes. However, when we do accept what is, even if it is hard, we open ourselves up to insight, ideas, and problem solving. We begin to finally make changes to restore peace. We allow ourselves to move through the pain and into the other side of the problem. Remember, you don't have to be 100% okay with the situation, you only have to see what is actually happening. Even though it is normal to wish for something else, these wishes will only cause you pain. When you accept what is, you are able to move forward from the point you are actually at.

Grief is one of the most avoided emotions. And who can blame anyone for wanting to resist it like the plague! But to avoid any emotion is to stuff it, and ignore it. And when you ignore your emotions, you are also ignoring the gift that the emotion brings when truly allowed to be felt and expressed. What you resist in yourself will persist. Yes, each painful emotion has something to teach us. They cultivate us, develop us, and we grow when we learn how to surrender to the power of our emotions. Begin to think of ignoring emotions as the same as resisting your growth. Surrendering doesn't mean lying down and being weak, it means that you pull from within you an inner strength that will assist you to feel, acknowledge, accept, and let go. It actually takes more courage to allow emotions to pass through you than to ignore or resist them because you are too scared to face and deal with them. When you surrender to your process of healing, all of the energy you have been using in resistance becomes available to you. Vitality, inner peace, harmony and most of all love are your rewards.

Hope: I once spoke to someone who went through a self help seminar that taught that the word "hope" is a bad word. They said that "hope is a pointless act. There is no hope, either you do something or you hope for it."As if hope would not lead you to take action. What if hope is actually the first action step?

I wondered if this person had ever been through an extreme dark time in their life. For me, hope is the first spark of light that occurs when we need it the most. Hope indicates that the sun is about to come out. It's like the morning star that assures you that darkness is lifting and beacons you to look higher and make a wish!

Hope is often sent to you by angels to open your heart to possibilities again. Hope is a beautiful, magnetic quality which attracts the great and wondrous into your life. There is no such thing as a pointless act and there is no such thing as staying stagnant in this ever expanding universe. There is always something going on, even if it is behind the scenes, and always a method to seeming madness. Hope itself is action, even if you cannot see the outcome of it yet. Hope is a verb, it is something you do. You are "doing something" when you are sitting around and hoping. Therefore, hope on any level cannot be a waste of time. Look for the star in the night that brings hope for a new day and go ahead.... Hope! Make a wish!

The Work

At some point, saying goodbye is something that will assist you in letting go. If your life suddenly changed you may not have had the chance to say goodbye or react in the way you wanted to. Giving yourself the opportunity to have a "second funeral," "break up ceremony," or a forgiveness ceremony of some kind can be very beneficial. Create a time and space for you to say things you weren't able to say at the time, or carry out appropriate actions that will help you to feel complete. For example, if you were in a relationship that ended abruptly due to the other person's actions, you may not have had a chance to get closure with the things you wanted to say and do. You can have a ceremony where you read a letter out loud to an understanding friend, God and your angles, or even to yourself- with the intent of finally letting them go. You can give yourself the closure you need.

There are probably things in your life right now that would be healthy to let go of. Perhaps a habit or addiction, or some negative fearful thoughts that have inhibited you from taking a life risk. Here is a process I have devised to help me release negativity I no longer want in my life. First, take a new notebook and inside of the first page write "Things That Must Go." Then write down all of the emotions, feelings, thoughts, beliefs, situations, circumstances, people, worries, concerns, fears, heartaches, grievances, anger, frustrations, and anything from your past, present, and future that you no longer want. Take your time with this list. Carry it around with you for at least a week. As negative or fearful thoughts arise, write them down. When you feel that you have dumped everything you are wanting or needing to let go of, take your list outside and burn it. Make sure to take a moment to look back over the pages and take note of any repeating phrases, thoughts, fears and worries. Notice your pain and honor yourself for what you have been through and what you are willing to let go of. As you cast the notebook into the fire, repeat these four sentences:

- I am sorry.
- Please forgive me.
- I love you.
- Thank you.

By repeating those phrases, you are cutting all ties, assuming accountability, and letting go in the spirit of forgiveness and love, which is the highest form of healing. You'll see a difference once you've completed this process. You might feel lighter, and that things are easing up for you.

28

Don't hesitate doing the entire process again and again as you shed the layers of things that must go.

The number one regret of the dying is that they did not live a life that was true to themselves. Can you imagine what it would feel like to lay on your deathbed knowing you could have done more? Ask yourself, what will you regret not doing when you are at the end of this life? Write down your answers and take a step towards making it happen right away.

Real Life

Often times it's not so much about what more you need to do, but what you need to let go of that makes the biggest improvement in your life. I worked for a business owner who was no different. She had hired me to be a coach for her employees and sales team, however I couldn't help myself- I ended up coaching her as well. One day, she arrived late to her office; make-up bag in one hand, breakfast in the other, hair still wet from her shower. She closed her office door so that she could finish getting ready for the day and be the boss for everyone who worked for her. As usual, she had her hands in every single thing she could possibly have her hands in. Her desk was chaos, her phone ringing under piles of papers. People were in and out of her office and it was impossible for her to focus on anything for very long before another distraction happened. I knew she was a mom of young children, a wife, and now the owner of a very busy and growing company, my heart went out to her. I wondered what she could do to get balanced. I had the opportunity to ask her just that one afternoon as I was sitting in her office- aka Grand Central Station. Finally, exhausted, she turned to me and asked, "What do I need to do?"

I replied to her question with a question, "What do you need to let go of?" Grand Central Station stopped. She stared at me blankly and repeated the question to herself. "I... I don't know...I can't let go of anything or nothing will get done!" Again I asked her a question, "Is everything getting done right now?" "No." was her honest reply. Then I asked, "Who can you delegate to?"

This began a process on a spreadsheet where she listed every one of her employees and every one of the company's tasks and began delegating like a queen running a country. I was so proud of her! Before long, she had removed over half of her responsibilities onto other people.

We also decided to close Grand Central by installing a secretary right outside of her door to monitor who could come and go from her office. She drew a large boundary with her time and space by learning how to let go of so much control and say "no" to doing everything. She began avoiding distractions which helped her to stay focused so she could complete one task at a time.

Letting go doesn't always have to be painful, sometimes it feels liberating to remove or delegate burdens, obligations, and distractions from our lives.

Archangel Azrael's Message To The Modern World: *"There is no right or wrong way to let something or someone go. Instead of attempting to control your emotions, which only creates more resistance and pain, try embracing and honoring what you feel. Give yourself permission to feel and be what comes naturally during the process of change. The idea that you have to be 100% all of the time is ludicrous and quite frankly it is dangerous. You can have a day where you're only 10% or even 0. In allowing yourself to process in your own natural way without the do's and don'ts, should and shouldn'ts, you allow yourself the gift of processing and growing in ways you would not in any other situation. I promise, there is a light at the end of every tunnel. I promise that you are never alone and that you will not face that light alone. At each end, there is indeed a glorious new beginning. The truth is, you never really stop going into the light.*

Remember that your love and comfort goes a long way. You will never put your own candle out as you light the candle of others; that's how light works. You have plenty of light to share with the world. Start lighting other people's candles!

Your loved ones who have crossed over are safe, happy, and still with you. Feel free to talk to them anytime you wish, and be open to seeing signs and feeling confirmation of their loving presence."

Questions To Consider: Are you someone who recognizes the signs of change, and moves fearlessly into the unknown or do you desperately and painfully hold on to things that have left your life? How do you honor your own grieving process? Can you put your own insecurities and discomfort aside and hold a quiet, solid space for someone who is grieving or do you shy away from others pain because you lack the words or skills to help?

Have you judged someone for grieving something you didn't think they had a reason to? How can you become a better listener? Who in your life right now could use your strong comforting presence? These are questions you want to ponder if you want to be like the solid, assuring, comforting Archangel Azrael.

Chapter 3

Archangel Chamuel- The Detective

What You Are Looking For Is Not Out There.

The hooves of a dark horse crash against the damp earth like thunder rolling across a barren field only to stop dead at the entrance of the forest. Their hunt- a white stag- has lost them entering the windy looming trees. Their breath, in unison is creating steam clouds around them in the cold air. The rider abruptly slides off of the horse and removes his helmet. He looks at his horse, then into the forest, then back to the horse who is nervously grunting and anxiously blowing more steam from his nose. It's the decision that he must make: Head into the unknown forest to find what he is searching for or turn around empty handed. He rubs the sweat off of his brow and holds his beating chest. It has already been a strenuous hunt. He has already come so far. He looks down at the ground and studies the thin grass growing through a patch of mud. At this point the pain of turning back would be too great. He turns around and stares into the open field and up into the sky. The clouds above are gathering; it will surely be a storm. His horse gives a loud impatient grunt. He is ready when his rider is. He has nowhere to go but into the forest. The forest is his new path, it is what he's prepared himself for. In a valiant motion down onto one knee, the rider quickly prays for guidance and protection. His horse steadies as he mounts him and once again turns to regard the past. And then it is there, a noise from the forest catches their attention and they both swing forward, catching a glimpse of the stag through the trees. The scent is inhaled into the horse's nostrils and his pupils grow wide. The rider firmly places his helmet back onto his head after flashing an adventurous grin. The chase is on and in an instant, the darkness of the forest envelopes the horse and his rider.

Archangel Chamuel is considered the "finding angel" and he is very much engaged in our insatiable search for something new. His name means "He Who God Sees." Archangel Chamuel's purpose and mission is to help us find what it is we are looking for whether it be our career, a soulmate, a new home, or more abstract things like our life purpose, inner peace, and motivation. However, nothing is too big or too small for this detective, he will even help you find your keys. Archangel Chamuel brings to light the adventure of new things. Like the rider in the description above, he reminds us that there is no turning back into our past. The unknown will one day become our known. He acknowledges the fear of doing something new, and he revels in the anxious excitement of taking the leap of faith. He reminds us that life without progression is death itself and that it is necessary to walk into the unknown if we truly want to live.

While the journey is exciting, you must also be grateful for what brought you to your present day endeavors. There will always be something that you can be searching and striving for. There will always be room for improvement, advancement and expansion. The balance is to appreciate what you have now while following your natural excitement for more. Archangel Chamuel reminds us that by appreciating what you already have, your journey for more can be filled with gratitude and happiness.

I heard a quote once that changed my entire philosophy on the journey. "Getting what we want is not the gift. Becoming who we need to become in order to get what we want is the gift." This reminds me of Archangel Chamuel, who rides alongside us on our search for our own illusive white stag. What we go through, how we develop ourselves, the talents and skills that we acquire while on the search is what makes us worthy of the kill. In a way, the stag (that which we are wanting) serves as our teacher and we are challenged, expanded, and cultivated in the journey until we are actually able to conquer it. The prize of any such journey is never what lies at the end of the road, but your own personal transformation that takes place along the way. You are your own reward, as the person you've become in the pursuit of your desires.

If Archangel Chamuel were human he would be a famous detective and his insight, wisdom, and enthusiasm for solving problems, riddles, and crime would make quite an impression on us all. Perhaps he would very publically share the thrill of each new adventure to find truth, clarity, justice, and peace. It would get us thinking about how we approach problems, riddles, and crime in our own lives. He would help us learn how to solve problems and find the truth about ourselves and the world around us. I chuckle to think that if he were human, Archangel Chamuel might even have his own reality show that paralleled crime shows like CSI, except he would actually teach ways to face our unknown answers head on with acceptance, problem solving strategies, and clear thinking. He would understand that finding answers to mysteries, solving cases, and bringing transparency to people brings closure and healing. He would be a blast to hang out with, always on the go, always onto the next adventure and searching for the next big mystery to solve.

In his spare time Archangel Chamuel would feel passionate about world affairs, as he is interested in helping us to find peace. He also might be a good matchmaker, as his knack for seeing patterns might help him sense who would be compatible with one another. He would most likely live in a city in Europe like London and he'd enjoy the diverse tourists and entertainment. His human self would sit at coffee shops, reading the paper, notebook in hand in case he needed to write down a new clue to his latest mystery. In his spare time, he would travel to mysterious places like Egypt and Machu Picchu. But at the end of the day, he would be well aware that whatever kind of enlightenment he received while discovering mysteries was already inside of him. He would simply enjoy the journey to finding his own wisdom within the inspiration of what was in front of him. While in his travels, he would make worldwide friends, taste the exotic foods of different cultures, and simply enjoy his journey. He would be an excellent story teller with all of his fun adventures and experiences. Every moment with him would seem like a new adventure whether you were talking about an exciting subject, trying something new, or discovering a newfound interest, food, or hobby that he introduced you to.

How You Can Be Like Archangel Chamuel

Start something. Now. That thing that you want to begin- do it! Jump in knowing that you can correct your course along the way. Be persistent. One foot in front of the other, one step at a time, you will reach your destination. Whether your "white stag" is a better looking body, more money, a stable relationship, success, more happiness, or a chance to travel the world, there can be a lot of distractions along the way that test your commitment, determination, and perseverance. The things you must learn on your way, when not understood as learning experiences, can sometimes discourage you. Depending on the goal, the journey can be a long, arduous roller coaster of achievements and seeming failures. You can be like Archangel Chamuel by deciding to stay on course and enter the dark forest NO MATTER WHAT.

I once heard that the word "Focus" is an acronym for Follow One Course Until Successful. This takes a lot of motivation. Think of motivation like a fire, and in order to keep a fire burning you need things to burn, right? There are two things in particular that will keep your fire burning: Commitment and perseverance.

"Searching is half the fun: life is much more manageable when thought of as a scavenger hunt as opposed to a surprise party."- Jimmy Buffett

The Mind State

Commitment: Commitment is staying focused on something you want to accomplish, after you have lost the drive to do the work. After all, commitment is different than being interested in something. When you are highly interested in something you'll do whatever is convenient. But when you are truly committed, you'll do whatever it takes for success. It's a good idea to ask yourself before getting involved with anything if you are truly committed or if you are just highly interested. This will help you determine where it is as a priority in your life.

When your commitment is being challenged, whether by others around you or by your own lack of motivation, think back to why you started in the first place. Get in touch with your "why." Once you remember why you started in the first place, your fire will begin burning again.

Perseverance: Perseverance is the ability to continue doing something when you feel tired, worn out, and run down. It's the internal overdrive that kicks into motion when you feel like quitting.

Perseverance requires practice. Just like a marathon runner, you must build your ability to go longer and harder over time. You do this by continually reaching your limits over and over until you learn how to go beyond them. Don't mistake building perseverance with burning out.

Burnout is when you go beyond your limits before you build perseverance.

A good thing to keep in mind while building your endurance levels- there's a difference between reaching up and stressing out. One feels like you're overcoming resistance, the other feels like you are abusing yourself. Even though you might be tired, building perseverance will always feel like you're accomplishing something.

When your perseverance is being challenged, reach for empowerment. Pat yourself on the back for the obstacles you've already conquered, and let those triumphs give you courage for challenges still to come. Celebrate your small accomplishments. Acknowledge you are doing more than you ever thought you would.

Adventure and Curiosity: Life is the ultimate adventure! You can cultivate this mind state by opening yourself up to the fact that the unexpected does and will happen, and it is okay. It is also okay to break old habits and ruts in which you are stuck. By exploring new things with a sense of excitement and courage, you will attract new and better opportunities and add a spirit of fun and renewal to your relationships.

Go ahead and let yourself be curious. Curiosity keeps you alive and radiant! You can never learn too much! No matter how old or experienced you are, you can be more curious about the world around you, the people around you, and the wonder-filled Universe in which you live. When you allow yourself to wonder and see life through the innocent, curious and adventurous eyes of a child, life will unfold for you it's many mysteries and you'll soon start believing in things you never dreamed of believing as a grown up!

The Work

Life is too short to not go where your heart leads you. Right now, write down what your heart longs for. What are you searching for? What does your "white stag" represent? Get very detailed, articulate, and clear about what you are really chasing.

Dig deep. When I opened my health clinic years ago, I thought I was chasing money and success. But my "white stag" turned out to be approval from my father. It was elusive and unattainable at the time and when I realized that the need for approval was driving me, all of the money and success didn't matter. I realized that I needed to just approve of myself, and let my father be who he is. This created a huge turn of events as the intentions for my health clinic turned into having a deep desire to help people heal.

Perhaps it has been a while since you have felt the excitement of a new dream to chase, or maybe you have never rode the horse of exhilaration while exploring some high set goals and if this is the case, it's time to saddle up! Take some time to look around you and within you to find something you want to go for. Maybe it's time to join a weight loss challenge, or take that class you keep putting off. What is something that you really want, but are too afraid to have? What is that thing that is out of your reach, elusive, and too hard to attain? That is your white stag! Go for it!

Your journey, whether it is towards a specific goal or a lifelong ride, is meant to be a thrilling and fun experience. When we become too serious and dead set on an outcome, we lose the sense of lightness, and things can become daunting. Even the most difficult journey can be eased when you see the funny side of things, so cultivate an appreciation for the ridiculous, the outlandish, and the silliness of life. Ask yourself right now how you can bring play, laughter, fun, and adventure into your social life, relationships, and work? Embrace the fun of learning, searching, and achievement.

Real Life

I remember the first time I realized that my favorite childhood fantasy, The Wizard of Oz was an actual work of wisdom. After Dorothy's world is hit with catastrophe she spins out of control in her house and wakes up in a new world. She then ventures out on a quest to return home that leads her to learn many things about herself. She bears witness to the development of a lion's courage, the deepening of scarecrow's knowledge, and the opening of a tin man's heart. She comes face to face with an illusion that scares her until it is finally revealed. She is mocked, captured, frightened, and abandoned. And at the end of this emotional rollercoaster, she is told that she had the power to return all along. But was her quest in vain? Had she known the power of her ruby shoes at the beginning of her quest, she wouldn't have developed so much of herself through all of the experiences in Oz. This story is not real life, however we are all living our own versions of Oz right at this moment. Our quests begin when chaos happens and we wake up in a world we don't belong in. We begin outside of our comfort zone, where everything looks and feel strange and scary. We search for ourselves, and a place we can call home again. Along the way, we face our worst fears and we learn that we really have what it takes to continue on down the yellow brick road. At the end of our quest, a new one begins as we click our heels together and transport into a new life, fully aware of new lessons. The next time you find yourself in Oz, outside of your comfort zone, scared, and searching for something remember that the power is within you all along the way. You just have to find it.

Archangel Chamuel's Message To The Modern World: *"Where is your sense of adventure? Did you leave it with your childhood dreams when you stopped playing? Have you grown to become limited, apprehensive, nervous and scared? The art of searching is a lost art. You now live in a society where everything is given to you instantaneously, and you are beginning to believe that anything you have to work or wait for is not worth it. It's the other way around; the things that require more effort on your part are of a much higher quality than any sort of instant gratification. Think about the important things in your life! You will never reach enlightenment overnight. You cannot microwave happiness. There is no instant coffee version of wealth. There is no magic pill to make someone fall in love with you, or give you the perfect body. There is no drive through that offers the kind of success you truly deserve. The time you spend wondering "what if" will surely eat your precious soul alive! You are meant to quest! There is simply no greater feeling than receiving the well deserved fruits of your labors! What is it you really want? Saddle up and get on your horse already! If you start today, a year from now, you will be glad you did! A year from now, what you will find is a much greater version of YOU because everything you want is within you. Go find it!"*

Questions To Consider: Are you tired of waiting for things to happen? Is there something you've wanted for a really long time, and the pain of not having it has ruined you in some way? What is your "white stag?" What resources will you need for your quest? What is your first step? Are you willing to do something every day to reach your goal? These are some things you might want to consider if you want to be like the fearless detective, Archangel Chamuel.

Chapter 4

Archangel Gabriel- The Messenger

Say What You Need To Say

She pulls her heavy cloak around herself tighter as the icy wind blows, hitting her face like pins and needles. Her black laced boots are soaked, muddy, and will look very worn after a long journey. She can hear the cavalry behind her; the wagon wheels as they crash into holes on the muddy path, the horse's hooves as they wearily make their way through the stormy hillside trail. Her army has gone silent, every man introverted, and engaged in his own mental battle to continue- to follow the woman who will lead them to freedom. Her legs beg her to cease but she must carry on. The message is too great, her mission is time sensitive, and she cannot spare a moment. In the attempt to ignore her body's cry for rest, she allows her mind to drift back to a time before she was made to be The Messenger- A time of warm fireplaces and rosy cheeked children playing by the hearth at solstice time. She lets her mind whirl with the music she loved to play on her simple flute while sitting in her garden on the long warm afternoons. She remembers her hot steamy bathing room where she would care for herself knowing that in doing so, she would have plenty to give to those she served. "Be sure to drink from the cup before you offer it," were the wise words from her mother. But that was a long time ago. She is now fulfilling her God-given mission to deliver the message at all cost. Through darkness, fear, deep freeze, and long restless nights, she stays her course following the morning star.

Archangel Gabriel is one of the more commonly known angels as she makes an appearance in the Bible as the angel who tells Mary of her destiny to bear the child of God. Therefore, she is often associated with delivering messages, childbearing, and pregnancy. Of course, the idea of pregnancy doesn't always have to do with having a baby. Pregnancy can be symbolically used to describe birthing/delivering a message, idea, abundance, or a creative project. When Archangel Gabriel is near, you will feel the gentle nudging to complete a project or deliver a message. Many artists, writers, and poets have admittedly felt an undeniable presence acting as a muse to birth their works of art.

Archangel Gabriel is often depicted in paintings with a long copper horn, harking good tidings and joy. Therefore, she is known as The Messenger. It is said that she and her messenger angels deliver the names of babies to their parent's ears.

Her assignment and purpose involves helping us with communication. She teaches that there are many ways to communicate and in most cases, the non verbal ways of communication can be the most powerful. Think of how powerfully Mozart communicated so many emotions through his music, or how an artist communicates a feeling through a painting or dance. We are not limited to only using words, yet we are not taught many other forms of communication. In some older cultures, simply looking into each other's eyes to relay the emotion within them was enough to create understanding and compassion. How often do we really communicate by looking right into each other's eyes? The expressions on our face and in our body language can tell us so much more than talking ever can. And then there is silence- probably the most powerful form of communication we have. Gabriel helps us understand these other forms of communication so that when we find we lack the words, we have other ways of communicating feelings and ideas.

With all of that said, it's important to understand that your words are still very powerful. They have the ability to break hearts and to start wars. Formulated in just the right way, words can produce the most eloquent poetry, soul connecting songs, and stories that take us to faraway places in our minds. When used with conviction, they hold the power to actually create anything we desire in our lives.

You are always communicating your wishes through the words you speak. Many times we talk about what we don't want. We complain about not having things we want and about situations that don't go the way we think they should. We saturate ourselves in negativity by gossiping, ranting, and engaging in the spreading of rumors, yet we are somehow surprised when we only receive more of those negative things in our lives. This is called a self-fulfilling prophecy. You don't necessarily get what you want- you get what you talk about. Whenever you complain about anything you are unconsciously tethering yourself to it. This is such a waste of power. Whatever you pour your energy into talking about is what will manifest for yourself every day. Are you creating happy self-made prophecies or ones you will surely regret? Archangel Gabriel helps to remain mindful of which reality to set up for yourself using your words as the roadmap.

If Archangel Gabriel were human, I believe she would be in control of her own television or internet station where she could bring to us unbiased, truthful, and insightful news and other programs. She would host artists and speakers who are here to celebrate wisdom, and art. She would challenge the current media by raising the bar and bringing productive information into our homes. She would be a force of truth to be reckoned with; however she would work mostly behind the scenes, allowing others to take the center stage and offer authenticity and honesty to the airwaves. She would work hard to raise the practice of integrity in our media and ask all of us to lower our tolerance for falsehood when it comes to the information we receive. She would remind us that we are all responsible for how much truth or untruth is passed around amongst us, and hold each of us accountable for the part we play in spreading information.

Archangel Gabriel would be a very professional, beautiful, powerful speaker. She would dress in simple and classy pencil skirts, slacks, and suit jackets and would be polished with sparkling copper jewelry to match her fiery copper hair. In her spare time she would enjoy reading the latest bestseller, walking through art museums, and attending live performances, enjoying all creative and unique forms of expression. She would surround herself with other "messenger angels" and you would find her attending parties with other reporters, writers, and artists. She would be a very upbeat, positive woman with an easy attitude towards the paparazzi. However, she would be very annoyed with anyone who gossiped, complained, or misused the art of communication and would be the first to call someone out who was attempting to spread obvious falsehoods. She would call you on your own negativity by asking you if that is really what you want to be focusing on. She would prefer to spend conversations finding solutions rather than dwelling on the problem.

She would be witty, funny, and you would hang on every word she spoke while she was telling a story. She would live near LA where she could be near the media but close enough to relax on a beach to get away from her work. She would constantly be writing, shooting pictures with her latest camera, and posting on social media. At the end of the day, she would kick off her shoes and sit by her fireplace to unwind with soft music and meditation.

How You Can Be Like Archangel Gabriel

For those of us who are inspired to share a specific message to the world, life at times can feel very much like the messenger at the beginning of this section. The burden of carrying the responsibility and the urgency to share your message can be both thrilling and scary. After all, our world is not known for the kindness it has shown towards messengers of the past. Ingrained in our memories are the lives and deaths of people like Joan of Arc, Jesus Christ, Martin Luther King, and many others who lost their lives at the hands of those who did not wish to receive their words. Today, we see less literal execution of messengers. The saying, "Don't shoot the messenger" is used as a joke. But we do see people being ridiculed and made fun of mercilessly by the media. Due to social media, it is even easier for complete strangers to post hurtful things that they may not otherwise say face to face. To put ourselves out into the world's view today takes as much bravery as ever before. To be willing to show your art, dance your dance, sing your song, preach your sermon, and to come out of hiding to give the world what your soul yearns to contribute takes a lot of guts. You may have to face the fact that you may not be everyone's cup of tea, but that is alright. You can be like Archangel Gabriel by fearlessly choosing to come out and show yourself to the world knowing that while you may gain some disapproval, you will always have your own self acceptance for doing what you were born to do. I love the saying, "If you want to put yourself out there to the world, you gotta have a thick skin and a short memory." My own life coach taught me that, and it has made it so much easier to embody Gabriel and express myself openly and honestly.

Whether you are feeling compelled to share a message with one person, or thousands, it takes a lot of energy to do it if you're worried about how the message will be received. Letting go of any expectations of people's reactions is key to sharing yourself authentically. Allow others their reactions, knowing that they do have a right to them, and detaching from the need to have their approval takes practice, but you'll get it once you start. It's an art to not let people's reactions to you drain you. I believe that is why Gabriel's message is to take care of you. She understands that in order to have what it takes to give to the world; you must drink from the cup first. Make sure you are giving yourself the approval and care that you need, that way you won't be so needy for it from others.

Archangel Gabriel stands to say that every life on this planet carries a message for the world, and this includes you too! In fact you may be sharing your message and may not even know it! There is a story of a man, who worked long hours at a job he disliked and every night on his way home he would want to stop at the liquor store and buy himself a drink, but he would walk by a homeless drunk and this reminded the man why he chose not to drink away his stress. Was this homeless man living out loud a very powerful message to those who were prone to become alcoholics? All we can know is that through his suffering, a very powerful message was relayed each day to keep others from ruining their lives through intoxication. Your life is your message. Is it telling the story you want the world to hear?

Archangel Gabriel as the messenger angel knows the importance of choosing the topics of conversation carefully so if you want to be like her, watch your words. Complaining is perhaps one of the worst forms of communication. It not only involves an extreme case of negativity, but it's one of the ways you can actually create horrible self fulfilled prophecies. You will inevitably get more of what you complain about. Complaining blocks all of your creativity, so it's impossible to get ideas, insight, or solve problems when you are busy complaining about them. STOP COMPLAINING ALTOGETHER! This one change in communication will change your life in monumental ways. By ceasing to complain at all, you are keeping your creative channels open and solutions, productive thoughts, and all of your artistic and creative endeavors will continue to flow.

"Everything becomes a little different as soon as it is spoken out loud." - Hermann Hesse

The Mind State

Authenticity: Who are the people who ridicule you? Who are the people you fear may say unsupportive things to you? Sadly, it can sometimes be the opinion of family or close friends that can deter you from being who you truly are, and having to renegotiate the closeness of those relationships can be painful as you begin to look for support from people who truly believe in you. As harsh as this is going to sound, letting go of the opinions of anyone who ridicules you is the absolute best thing you can do. Sometimes we think certain people will react to us a certain way. We are so sure of what they are going to say that we can already hear their voice in our heads, and we are so convinced by what they "say" that we will go to great lengths to avoid their seemingly inevitable judgment altogether. However, these assumptions may not ever come to pass, and so the pain and strife we go through on the basis of things not actually happening can make you feel insane. You'll never know how someone is going to react to you until you actually give them the opportunity to react. Until then, you are making up scary stories in your head that keep you from being authentic.

I had a very hard time coming out of the "angel closet" and admitting to people that I can see, hear, and feel angels. I had this idea that people who talked to angels had to wear hippie clothes, never wear makeup or take showers, and be poor. A lifestyle I certainly don't condemn, but it's just not me. I was so afraid I wouldn't be taken seriously, and that I would be laughed at by my peers and mentors. I was afraid that my religious family would judge me. But I had to finally face the fact that there is nothing in the world I would rather do than to help people connect to angels. I became okay with my gifts and the kind of lifestyle I wanted to have. I had to fall in love with myself, and avoid anyone who validated my fears that I was weird and worthless. My authenticity sprang forth when I realized and accepted who God created me to be. Once I was able to admit it to myself that I was His beautiful, unique, quirky, loving creation, and that this was my Divine purpose in life, it no longer mattered what anyone could say to me. I was able to shout from the mountain tops, "Hey! I'm THE Angel Lady! I'm brilliant when it comes to angels! In fact, I'm a total expert when it comes to angels! Talking and teaching about intuition and connecting to angels is my passion, my purpose, my dream! AND I don't have to look a certain way. I love shopping, wearing makeup, living lush, and I deserve to be respected as a professional!" I'm not afraid to be me. My thoughts, beliefs, words, and actions all line up, and that is what makes me authentic.

Just like how I had to step into my authenticity and admit and embrace my message, I know that you also have something that you could be an expert in. There are no "chosen ones." Each and every one of us has a personal genius. You just have to find yours. Express yourself and what you are you're good at, no matter how quirky or unpopular you think it might be. People always love seeing the genius of others. You will inspire many by living in your truth!

Creativity: How willing are you to consider new ideas, concepts, and experiences? Creativity requires you to think with an open mind and consider things outside of the box. For instance, a painter may consider what else a blank canvas would look like. A dancer will consider what else her body can do. For myself, this book was a creative expression of my original thought, "How can we all be like the angels?" Being open to possibilities is like wafting air into your own inner creative spark that becomes a fire of burning desire to express itself.

Creativity is the open door to change, and since most people are afraid of change, they stifle their creativity. If you want to be more creative, consider a playful approach to a problem. Begin a stream of "what if" statements and see where your imagination can take you. Creativity is often accompanied by having fun. Having fun, laughing, and indulging in a good time can open you up to new ideas and inspirations, and help you to feel safe with any changes your creative imagination might entice you to make.

The Work

Listening is the most important part of communicating. In every conversation you participate in it is important that you really pay attention to the other person. Don't just think about what you will say next as they are talking. Learning how to enter the space with another with precision- completely conscious and with the understanding that you are there to listen and hear them. Before interactions ask yourself, "How am I entering this conversation? Do I have any malice, unaddressed feelings? Where is my peace? Where is my power? Is my judgment or perception of this person creating a block?" This kind of conscious interaction creates precision and will change the way all of your interactions take place. Some of the most powerful people I have met in my life had a way of making me feel like I was the only person in the room. They were precise with their attention, and I left feeling special and important. These interactions showed me that it is possible and as I myself have put this into practice and to focus 100% on the person in front of me, I find that it is much like a meditation, where I have the opportunity to push aside distractions for the sake of being 100% present with another person.

Everything around you is also constantly communicating. Take the time and listen to what the world around you has to say, and pay attention to what kinds of messages you are allowing to permeate your life. Listen to good music, listen to children, and listen to nature. Find positive and uplifting people to follow on social media and allow only good and positive messages to be relayed to you all day long. Remove those negative messages that the world constantly throws your way in the form of doom and gloom news, gossipy magazines, drama filled TV shows, and violent movies. Listen to your mind, and be willing to replace any negativity that pops up with a positive affirmation. You can dramatically change your life by simply filling your world with beautiful uplifting sounds.

What is your favorite word? It's a funny question, and perhaps you have never chosen a favorite. Play around with different words and really feel what they mean to you. When you find a word that makes you feel really good, spend 5 minutes just meditating on that one word. Say it slowly, let each letter and syllable roll off of your tongue. Words are very powerful, and when you find one that centers you, remember it. Write it down somewhere and say it often. Use this practice when you are stressed out and need to get centered again. Example- if the word "harmony" or "tranquility" gives you a settled feeling, say it slowly while taking deep breathes next time you need that feeling.

Gratitude is the medicine to all discord. If there is anything you take away from this chapter, let it be the truth of that statement. The answer to most every challenge you will face in life is contained within the depths of your gratitude. If you want your creative juices to really flow, and if you want to overcome the challenges in your life, start a gratitude journal. The key to being grateful is identifying the things for which you are blessed, even in times of struggle. Every day, write a list of these blessings and be sure to include why you are so thankful for them. The more you practice this record of gratitude, the more your list will grow with each day. Start with just 10 things you are most grateful for each day and why and you will begin to see how rich and blessed your life truly is.

Real Life

Years ago, I was an X-ray technician at a medical family practice. I loved how my office was away from the nurse's stations and billing offices. It was quiet and separated from the office drama, gossip, and cattiness, of which there was always plenty. There was one woman in particular who really loved to stir the pot and spread gossip. She was an older lady who worked in the collections department. She was picky, critical, and mean, and on a daily basis I would go out of my way to avoid her. I of course knew nothing about her personally, other than she looked absolutely miserable and had a horrible reputation for backstabbing and complaining about everyone- even the patients!

One day she came into my lab wearing a patient gown and coughing like crazy. Apparently, she had not been to work for a few days, and the Doctors we worked for insisted that she come in for a checkup. When they had seen her symptoms, they sent her to me for a chest x-ray. At first, I rolled my eyes. I did not want to be interacting with this malicious woman for one second. I got her situated and prepped for the x-ray by asking her the normal intake questions and getting the room and camera ready. Then I noticed her face. She was drawn, quiet, and seemed very distraught. I stopped what I was doing and really looked at her. When I asked her if she was okay, I held my breath waiting for an insulting reply, but instead I got something completely different. "I'm scared." She said helplessly looking down at her hands. "And you're about to see me naked, and I don't like that either."

I smiled and sat down across from her on the table. "You can leave the gown on, it's an x-ray," I said lightly. "And it's okay to be scared. Most people are scared when they come into this dark room. What are you most scared about?"

"I'm scared that this isn't just a cough. I've been feeling off for months. I'm scared it's something worse, and I'm scared I'm going to die alone because I don't have anybody." Then out of seemingly nowhere, there were tears. Tears on my table from this woman as she spoke her truth out loud. I realized she felt very alone. I was suddenly in an awkward position because I felt like reaching out, but she was like a wounded animal- I had no idea how she might react to the kindness. Would she bite my caring hand out of her usual bitterness as I expected she might?

"You're not alone right now. I'm here and we'll get you through this. A few photos and we'll know exactly what's going on." I spoke slowly and kindly hoping my encouraging words would not be rebuked. To my surprise, she solemnly nodded her head and we proceeded with the X-rays.

Later in the developing room, my heart sank as I watched her x-rays emerge from the processor. I could clearly see irregular and abnormal shadows on the lung fields indicating harmful masses. This was not a simple chest cold. "Dammit." I said under my breath.

I saw the look on the Doctor's face as I placed her x-rays on the light board. We shared a glance that confirmed we saw the same thing. He released her from work for further testing, rest and treatment. I didn't see her again for many weeks after that.

Then one day, as I was wiping off the exam table I looked up and saw her in my doorway. She wore a serious expression and I put down my spray bottle and towels to motion for her to come in.

I was surprised by the low hoarse tone of her voice as she spoke to me. "I just wanted to thank you for being so kind to me when I was in here last. I don't think I've ever been so nervous in my entire life, and the words you said to me were so comforting. Thank you."

I was speechless and nodded my head. She continued, "It really made me think about why I am so alone. I don't think I've ever said caring things like that to another person, not even my cat. I never realized that a lot of the people who come into this office are scared like I am. I don't want to be like that anymore."

Again, I was silent but I felt my eyes show understanding as I nodded again. "Anyway," she coughed into a tissue and finished, "I just want to thank you for showing kindness to me when I didn't deserve it."

"You are welcome." I simply said and we shared a smile before she was gone. I never knew what became of her because I ended up taking a job in another office shortly after the interaction. But, I've often thought back to how someone was able to change the way they spoke by just being heard, understood, and spoken to kindly. By speaking her truth and admitting she was scared it allowed me to communicate what she needed to hear the most. I find it endearing to know that sometimes it's the simplest dialogues that create profound shifts in people.

Archangel Gabriel's Message To The Modern World: "*Everything you hear and talk about affects you deeply. If you want to know where you will be in a year from now, look at what books you read, shows and movies you watch, social media you play in, music you listen to, and people you surround yourself with. If you are surrounding yourself with negativity and drama, you will become negative and your life will mirror this with unnecessary drama. The best way to improve your life, become happier and more successful at anything you do is to dial up! Focus your attention where you want to be and how you want to feel. Listen with love- speak with love. And when you feel ready to share your message to the world, you will already be involved in communities and a container that will support you! Sing your song, write your book, play your instrument, dance your dance, speak your words, cook, create, build, generate, produce, manufacture, invent, discover, make and communicate with the world! Share it with one or millions, we need you!*"

Questions To Consider: In what ways do you need to learn how to communicate better? Do you feel compelled to create something? Is it time to go on a "negativity detox" and rid your life of negative media? Who are your supporters? Do you need to let certain naysayers go from your life? How well do you enter the space of another with precision? These are some questions you may want to consider if you want to be a leader in communicating like the clear spoken Archangel Gabriel.

Chapter 5

Archangel Haniel- The Mystic

Love Changes Things

The sky is clear, the stars are out. The full moon is rising over the dark mountain silhouette in the east. The air wraps itself around you like a cool blanket and your shoulders relax as you inhale the sweet floral scent of the night. There in front of you, she beckons you to come forward. Through the high stone walls, under an archway of roses, and into her garden you approach her reverently and humbly. Everything is bathed in the bright blue moonlight, making it seem as though you have entered a place of magic. The lightning bugs twinkle in the air like heavenly stars, and you take it all in with wonder and awe. You have no idea why you have come here, but her eyes rest upon you as though she does. Her gaze mesmerizes you, and with every moment you are more sure she knows you. She leads you to a stone well where she effortlessly draws up the bucket, dips her simple goblet into the shimmering water, and gracefully offers the full cup to you. You step up to her slowly, never taking your eyes off of her, and now aware of your dry mouth you accept the goblet from her hands and lift it to your lips. You drink in the mineral rich liquid and you feel it quench every cell in your body. As you hand the goblet back to her, you begin to notice your eyesight become clearer. You notice her silver hair and white robes are glowing. Her skin is bright in the moonlight. And her eyes... they are taking you in, enveloping you in a love you have not understood before. Something opens in your chest, as though you have a third lung, inhaling, expanding. You are calmly aware that you are changing right in this moment, you are aligning to something, you are shedding, unraveling, shifting, growing, becoming...

Unconditional; to be loved deeply without condition- a sensation you have never understood before this moment...

Love changes things. I have come to know that anything or anyone I pour my love into becomes different after I have touched it. In a world filled with conditions, rules, restrictions, and limits, love comes in to free us, to unbind us, and to liberate us. While we might presume to master our many emotions, selecting and manipulating them to our desires, love instead has its own way with us. We do not control love, and the things we do in order to grasp it, label it, control it, or deny it often leads us to suffering. Love is indefinable, uncontrollable, and the most mysterious, feared, and sought after thing in the universe. That is because love is not to be understood-in fact it cannot be understood- only accepted.

"The heart wants what the heart wants," is a saying that we helplessly use to try and define why we love. Love represents all the parts of us that are completely out of our control: our true passions, our true desires, our magnificence, our gifts, our inhibitions, our spontaneous wild nature. And just like how we suffer when we attempt to squelch love, we destroy ourselves when we deny these parts of us we cannot understand. Like love, these parts of ourselves are not meant to be understood- just accepted.

We live in a world governed by the mind, and the mind has the need to understand, qualify, label, and organize what it sees. Love, does not fit in the mind's world. However, when we are fearless enough to bring love in its fullest expression into our lives, it changes things. To the mind, this change is chaos. But love is the language of God and Nature, both of which are ever expanding. Love is the mystery; it doesn't need to be known by the mind- it is to be felt with the heart.

Archangel Haniel is the Archangel who embodies the essence of love's great mystery. Her name means, "Grace of God. She is an extremely feminine angel who would be most closely related to the feminine aspect of God; Divine Feminine, Heavenly Mother, or Goddess. She represents the natural cycles and rhythms of the moon, the earth, and ourselves. Yes, we all do cycle- even men. There are times we may feel very outgoing and active, and other times when we may feel more introverted and withdrawn. It is normal to have ups and downs, in and outs, dark times and light times.

In honoring cycles, Archangel Haniel mostly reminds me of the moon. Unlike the sun, which is constant in his rising and falling each day, the moon is a very unruly heavenly body. She rises at different times, looking different with every appearance. Sometimes she is visible during the day, other times we don't see her at all. She is far less obvious than the sun- of whom you can tell is out even when you're inside of a building. But the moon...where is she? What is she doing now? She has her own way with the skies. However, if you were to track and study her you would see that there is a definite method to her seeming madness. She has a definite rhythm and follows a consistent cycle. Hers is just less obvious than that of the sun. The other quality I like to point out about the moon is that she is purely receptive. The only reason she glows is because she reflects the light of the sun. Such is the nature female energy: while male energy is predominantly giving, female energy is receptive. Archangel Haniel is here to remind us that in order to give light, we must receive it first. She's also here to remind us that while we may have parts of ourselves that are very much like the sun -- consistent, hard-working, outgoing, and giving, we also have parts of ourselves that are like the moon--cyclical, introspective, quiet, and receptive. It is important to honor and balance both qualities. What you give, you will receive back; what you receive you will naturally give. There is a great security in knowing that love flows equally in both directions. Think of it like breathing. There is plenty of love, like there is plenty of air and in order to thrive we must find the balance of inhale and exhale. When we learn to live like this love becomes a priceless asset.

Archangel Haniel would be a very magical human. She would look like a goddess and wear flowy clothing and crystals around her neck. She would radiate deep wisdom. Professionally, she would work as a natural medicine doctor with herbs, homeopathy, and natural hormone therapy replacement for men and women who want to balance their physical cycles, stress, and aging process. In her spare time she would find pleasure in ballet and modern dance where she would be posed, skilled, emotional, and filled with grace.

I do believe she would be a private person, and perhaps practice the old magic of Avalon (communing with nature to help restore peace to earth) behind closed doors. She would spend a lot of time in prayer, knowing that by pouring her love into world affairs and harsh situations, her love is mighty enough to create change.

She would be elegant, beautiful, and refined, and men would most likely be both extremely intrigued and scared of her. It is intimidating to be loved by a person who knows the power of love. She would not buy into the idea that we should ever restrict our love. She would live with her heart wide open because she knows that in her vulnerability is her strength. In her unwillingness to fold or shrink at the opportunity to change someone with her love, she would do whatever it took to learn and grow, to break down whatever walls kept her from giving all of her heart. She would build her endurance, baring all, challenging fear itself until it found no place in her holy presence. She would face the fears of rejection and judgment like the moon faces the world each time it rises; sometimes dark, sometimes full, but more often somewhere in between. And always, always in her perfect time, in the silent honor of which she is, and the magic that is both her light and her darkness.

It is hard to define this angel as a human as I have the others. It is like attempting to define love- while centuries of writers have attempted, and some have come close, we all know that they have come short to define the indefinable. The moment we open ourselves to receive love, it transforms us, and that transformation is the closest thing that can be used to describe love. It simply changes you. This is the message Archangel Haniel brings into this world.

How You Can Be Like Archangel Haniel

Archangel Haniel is magic. She is patient. She is kind. She is understanding, compassionate, and wise because she knows how to listen to her heart. And to tell you the truth, you are already like her when you allow yourself to be open and receptive. The unkind, harsh, unloving, judgmental version of you is simply like the shadow the earth casts upon the moon.

Shadows are simply the parts of us that aren't lit with awareness, love, and acceptance. They are the little cries for love within our minds that worry, judge, and fear the worst. They are an accumulation of our unresolved pasts, hurts, and thoughts that became distorted during times of hurt and loss. These thoughts were decisions we may have made about ourselves when we were feeling down, that aren't necessarily true. Archangel Haniel is not afraid to question her darker thoughts and beliefs about herself and the world around her. If you want to be like her, you too can begin to shed light upon your own shadows by acknowledging that shadows are simply the lack of light and that the best remedy for them is the light of love. Love your shadows, love yourself when you are afraid, stressed out, irritated, worried, and insecure. This love will bring the full moon's light into the darkness of your mind and lead you home.

"Being deeply loved by someone gives you strength, while loving someone deeply gives you courage." -Lao Tzu

The Mind State

Openness: Love has never been the cause of your suffering and pain. But it is the lack of love, or the resistance to love that has caused much hurt. Love is medicine, it is our life energy. Anytime you have perceived a reason to withhold love, you feel pain. You may even feel that if there is no one around to pour your love into that you must withhold your love-and this causes you more pain. Loneliness is not about another person as much as it is the feeling of not having love in your life. You are lonely for love. However, you do not have to be with another person in order to experience love. Love is your birthright and is not conditional upon you being with another. Again, it is like air, you must breathe it in, and breathe it out. Just as you can inhale right now while reading this, you can also decide to open your heart and feel love. Right now, try it.

Honoring Cycles: You may feel love cycle like the moon. Sometimes it rushes in and through you like the brightest light in a wild sky full of stars! Other times, love may be quiet, still, reverent and hushed. Your sensitivity levels may cycle too. Sensitivity is simply a form of awareness. When you feel overly sensitive, it is because your awareness is heightened and it is time to pay attention to something and make changes. Learning how to honor your natural rhythms and cycles keeps you from judging yourself or thinking there is something wrong with you when you feel different from one day to the next.

At the core of your being, you are a living organism just like everything else on this earth. You are responding to the world around you, growing, retracting, and moving as a part of a natural life cycle. Once you know this about yourself, you will be able to foresee times when you may not be so outgoing and prepare for this part of your cycle. For instance, as a creative person, I know that I have waves of ideas and energy. Sometimes I'm a social butterfly and I flit around making my presence known. Other times, I want to stay close to home and wear slippers all day. However, I like to stay consistent for my followers and clients so I work on preparing my blogs, classes, and coaching when I am in a work mode cycle. I wrote 20 blog posts before I ever launched my blog site so that if there was a week I didn't particularly feel like writing, I could just post one I already had on hand. My classes and lesson plans are already planned out and ready to be taught so that no matter where I am in my cycle, I can deliver amazing content. Expecting to be a shining bright full moon every day is unrealistic and it leads you to judge yourself when you're feeling more like a dark new moon. So, let yourself off the hook, prepare yourself for when you're feeling more introverted and quiet, and honor wherever you are in your natural cycles.

Patience: I love the phrase, "patience is pretty." It's true, every time you become impatient, you can act ugly! Think back to a time when you were rude or aggressive because you felt impatient. Or think about how your boss or a parent acts when they are impatient. People become mean, harsh, hurtful, relentless, and extreme when they are forced to wait against their will. We can sometimes take our impatience out on others. We then complicate the situation further due to irrational actions and can make ourselves look foolish to those around us. This kind of behavior can lead us to feel embarrassed later when we realize how ridiculous we were acting. These are not the graceful ways of Archangel Haniel. You can honor the dark parts of yourself, acknowledging your impatience, while still practicing patience. This is why it's called "practicing patience." Take a deep breath, go for a walk, and focus on something else. When you do this, things will run smoother, quicker, and without the drama and hurt feelings. Patience is a skill to master and it requires you to learn self discipline and trust. Whenever life asks you to wait, trust that you're being prepared for something even better than you expected. All things happen at the perfect time, and this can be hard to accept when it's not happening when you wish it would. Begin to train yourself to relax and become calm when you feel impatient. When your thoughts and actions are sweet, patient, and pretty, you'll be able to clearly receive guidance, ideas, and instruction on what is really going on and what you can do while you're waiting. When the time is right, and you are ready and refreshed, the door will open and things will move forward.

The Work

To live with an open heart is to be fearless. Love is not for the faint of heart! In fact, every one of us lives behind a list of reasons and excuses to justify our closed heart. The first step is to take a look at your heart. I highly suggest writing down all of your fears, excuses, and justifications for not being more open to love. It's very powerful to look at the reasons why you've closed yourself off to love or being loved on paper. Perhaps someone has hurt you or taken advantage of you. Maybe you view your heart as weak. You may only be seeking to protect yourself, but staying closed off to your natural state of being open, accepting, and loving is what will do you the most harm. Once you have your reasons in front of you, write this question and really ponder it before answering it: "What does my heart long for?" Taking an honest look at your heart is liberating as you free yourself from any denial, walls, and resistance to love. If you want to be like Archangel Haniel, it's time to acknowledge your true desires about love and release your fears that are holding you back from them. Have the courage to love, and you will find that your heart is actually very strong!!

Giving love doesn't mean being a doormat, it doesn't make you a servant, it doesn't make you weak. It does make you vulnerable, it does make you humble, and it will give you compassion. Sometimes love will ask you to do things that go against the norm. Sometimes it will tell you to be tough. It will tell you to be silent when you want so badly to lash out, and it will tell you to be brutally honest when you want to save feelings. Love will tell you to take action when you want to hide away. But love always knows what you need. You may not understand it in the moment, but it serves to bring correction and grace into your life and the lives of others. When you allow love to speak through you instead of your fears, your authenticity will shield you from others attacks and accusations. Honest love will cut through layers of lies and deceit to the heart of any conflict. To always choose love above being right, above being safe, above being scared, that is the magic of life. Master that, and you will have an idea of what it is like to embrace the uncontainable and live within the mystery.

Avoid burnout by allowing yourself a day off on a regular basis. Pay attention to your body and your mind when they begin to show signs of needing some down-time. Instead of judging yourself as weak, tired, stressed, or rundown, recognize it as a time where you need to receive. Perhaps you've been excessively giving, and it is time to care for yourself and/or allow others to give back to you. Honor other people's cycles. Recognize when someone is feeling more introverted and quiet and give them space when it is time for them to rest and rejuvenate.

Love itself often requires that you do work you don't necessarily want to do, however it is work that shapes you and redefines you into a better person. Sometimes it will require you to put yourself last, and other times it will ask you to put yourself first. Love is an unruly teacher; kind yet strict and unrelenting with her intentions of shaping you into a better human being.

Here are a few lessons I have received from love that were hard, yet powerfully transforming. As you go through these ideas, consider writing down your own personal feelings, experiences, or thoughts.

1. **You are not responsible for how others feel.** As a notorious people pleaser, this was a hard lesson for me. The ability to speak up, do the things you need to do, and be who you are without needing the approval of others is a huge act of self love. You cannot make anyone feel anything, and the highest form of love is accepting another person's feelings regardless of how they may affect you.

2. **Loving does not mean fixing.** There are actually people who believe it is their job to fix people, and they are naturally attracted to people they think need rescuing. In trying to fix another person they receive a sense of accomplishment and feel that their life has meaning. But in truth when we focus on fixing others in the name of "love" we are robbing them of their personal power to save themselves and feeding the illusion that they are damaged. Fixing people is a form of avoidance from our own issues because we focus more on the other person's problems rather than our own. No one is broken and no one needs fixing. We are all on a journey. You cannot protect someone from an outcome they have created in order to learn something. Love means that you are

there to comfort and support them while holding a firm knowing that they are perfect, and that their journey is perfect for them.

3. **Holding space for another.** This is a huge lesson because it requires inaction. It requires that you just simply listen and show up as a strong non-judging, unconditional, powerful space for another person. I learned this while helping women overcome abuse at a women's convention. Allowing them to cry and scream it out, without rushing over to comfort, without offering words of healing, without interrupting their process at all- but to just be there with my heart open sharing tears and creating a safe place for them to heal themselves. Holding space for another person is empowering because more often than not, people know how to self correct- they just haven't had the environment and uninterrupted support in which to do it in.

4. **Self Love.** Knowing how to show up for yourself in loving ways is imperative to your growth. It's necessary to break through your fears of becoming selfish or narcissistic when showing yourself love. Self love is not egotistical. You cannot truly care for others if you haven't learned how to care for you. In other words, you will live your life completely perplexed at why people don't show up for you until you learn how to show up for yourself. People who love themselves are fun and easy to be around, they attract happy and positive people, and they tend to avoid relationships that are codependent and draining. People who love themselves become confident and make decisions based on their self love. So, make sure you are giving yourself all of the love you need.

5. **Distant love.** Love is something that is not contingent upon time or space. You are free to love that which is not right next to you. You can love the hungry children in other countries, you can love the rainforests, and you can love someone who lives far away from you. You can continue to love people who have crossed over. As I stated earlier, love is not bound like we are. It is free to go wherever it wants, and will go wherever you direct it. And because your love changes things, don't hold back. Love everyone everywhere and any time you feel the need to love. Send it out into the world and watch things change.

6. **Love your teachers.** Some people will come into your life for a moment, others will stay a while, and some people will walk by your side for a lifetime. These are your teachers. Sometimes they hurt you, and you are left learning. Sometimes they lift you up,

and you are still left learning. Love the people who have taught you either through pain or pleasure. They are your teachers.

In order to understand the next section, I wanted to share a beautiful quote from one of my favorite books.

> "My wife and I just don't have the same feelings for each other we used to have. I guess I just don't love her anymore and she doesn't love me. What can I do?"
> "The feeling isn't there anymore?" I asked.
> "That's right," he reaffirmed. "And we have three children we're really concerned about. What do you suggest?"
> "Love her," I replied.
> "I told you, the feeling just isn't there anymore."
> "Love her."
> "You don't understand. The feeling of love just isn't there."
> "Then love her. If the feeling isn't there, that's a good reason to love her."
> "But how do you love when you don't love?"
> "My friend, love is a verb. Love - the feeling - is a fruit of love, the verb. So love her. Serve her. Sacrifice. Listen to her. Empathize. Appreciate. Affirm her. Are you willing to do that?"
> — Stephen R. Covey, The 7 Habits of Highly Effective People: Powerful Lessons in Personal Change

Real Life

I was coaching a woman who was at the end of her rope with her husband. He suffered from depression and slept a lot. According to her, he would get up, smoke weed, eat, and then go back to bed. He hardly worked and she felt overwhelmed with financial responsibility and feeling alone and unsupported in the relationship. I asked her what kind of support she was offering him. She went silent and then began to defend herself: "Support? I'm supposed to support him while he's being like this? This isn't the man I married, I've been ripped off, and you really think it's me who should be supporting him? He should be off of his butt supporting me! After all I'm doing everything to make things work!"

I gently asked, "What are you doing to make things work between the two of you?" Again she was silent and then defensive. "Well I can't condone his behavior. I don't know what's going on with him, but he needs to get better. He should be working, he should be interacting with me, he should be helping out around the house!"

As I listened I realized that she had entered what I call the "should" zone. The "should zone" is deadly to any relationship that wants to thrive. As soon as you begin using the word "should" towards your partner, you enter a zone of judgmental finger pointing and negative, unproductive attacking. As long as you are "shoulding" on anything, you are focusing more on your unfulfilled wishes and desires than on what is actually happening. No solutions or answers come from "shoulding." If you want things to change, you have to accept what is going on in the here and now. In fact, I suggest that you remove the word "should" from your vocabulary all together. It doesn't mean you have to be okay with what is going on, but you have to see and accept that it is happening. From this point of accepting what is happening, you are able to find solutions. When you release expectations, you are free to enjoy things for what they are, instead of what you think they should be.

I asked my client, "How would this situation change if you decided to pour your love into it? How do you think your husband, in his depressed state would respond if you totally accepted him 100% for who he is right now, doing what he is doing? I'm not saying you have to be okay with it, it's okay to not be okay with it, you get to have and honor your feelings. However, what do you have to lose by turning your heart on and just simply allowing your natural feelings towards him- the ones beneath the judgment and "shoulding"- to emerge? What do you think would happen if you just loved him and showed him you love him regardless of what he is or isn't doing?"

It was then when my client began to cry. These were tears that had been held hostage inside of her heart by her anger and resentment towards him. Once I told her that her feelings were okay and normal AND she could still love him, her true feelings for the man she loves rushed forward. After a long tear-filled discovery session with me, she agreed to try it. To tell you the truth, I had no idea what would happen with my guidance. When you're dealing with love, anything can happen. I hoped with her, for the best.

Two weeks later I received a text from her. She told me that it took her a few days to really let go of her expectations for what her husband should be doing, but once she let go, it was actually easier to just let her love flow. She found herself wanting to lay by him while he slept during the day. She found herself crying in his arms. Somehow her tears found their way past his stoned mind one day and he woke up and cried with her. No words were ever spoken, but from that moment on, she poured her love into the food she prepared for him, into his laundry she folded and put away. She poured her love into the way she kissed him each morning and night. She stopped nagging and ragging on him about what he should be doing. She let him off the hook and simply yet powerfully showed her love and care for him. After 2 weeks, her husband got out of bed, put his work clothes on and went to work. She poured her love into the meal she had ready on the table for him when he came home that night. She poured love into her fears that he wouldn't do the same thing the next day. She poured love into her wounds, her disappointments, self righteousness, and into her expectations. Her heart was finally in charge and it had enough love to heal them both. This man grew under love's spell. He woke up from his hell in a sea of love. Love, in its purest form, transformed them both.

When someone we love enters the dark part of their lives, we can either react from fear or from love. One is the terrorist, one is the healer. The next time you want to become scared over what your loved ones are doing, ask yourself what would happen if you just accepted and loved them. How would love transform you all?

And finally, if you are pouring your love onto someone or into something and this has transformed you, but the person or object has rejected the medicine that love can bring, then this is a sure sign that your love can be focused somewhere else. We all have free agency, and sadly some people are determined not to thrive under love's power. Those people need to heal and do their own work so that they aren't just taking advantage of your love, or being threatened by it, or challenging it. One of the biggest lessons I've learned when it comes to my heart is that I know exactly what I will do for love. And while I believe there is plenty of love to give to everyone I meet, knowing what I will do for love in a relationship has made me very selective of whom I share my heart. I know my love is powerful AND I know that my love can still be rejected. I know that my love changes things AND I know that there are people who resist the natural flow of love's correction. I have witnessed the greed, selfishness, and rejection that come from unhealthy intentions and beliefs towards love. I have also seen myself and lovers transform within love's care. Love is powerful. Use it largely, and use it wisely.

Archangel Haniel's Message To The Modern World: *"The moon, in her magnificence holds so much wisdom and insight for you if you would only notice her. What the moon does when you cannot see her is the same as she does when she lights up your sky, the only difference is the shadow that is cast upon it. This is the same with your shadows. Just because you may be feeling dark, misunderstood, and unloved, doesn't mean that any of that is true. Under the layers of those shadows, you are still bright and magnificent. Just as the new moon fades into a full moon, whatever shadows you are experiencing right now will pass. Remember who you are under the darkness, and remain poised, centered, and graceful. Everything will be okay.*

Let love in, allow it to teach you and to guide you. The more love you use and give, the more you will be given. The supply of love is endless. Allow love to pour into you and heal any part of you that is crying for love. In doing so, you will be able to pour your love into others, and this will heal the world!

Questions To Consider: What changes does your heart want you to make? What sort of cycle are you in right now? Is it time to celebrate your light, or honor your darkness? In what area of your life do you wish you were more silent and graceful? How can you embrace and accept the mystery and love? Who needs your love? At the end of the day, what are you willing to do for love? These are questions you want to ask yourself if you want to be like the ever powerful love filled, magical mystic, Archangel Haniel.

Chapter 6

Archangel Jeremiel- The Counselor

Mistakes Are Proof You are Trying

The shocking sight of her made everything start spinning. The sudden onset of anxiety made his stomach lurch into his throat and he desperately tried to swallow. The rush of blood to his face, the instant sweat that formed on every inch of his body told him that he should panic. But his mind was kicking in like a proud wounded animal telling him, "no, no, no, you will NOT run, you will stand tall!" He gripped his bag with a trembling hand squared his shoulders and cleared his throat. Had it really been 2 years since he had seen her face? Her hair was different, she was dressed in new clothes, and she was walking nonchalantly down the opposite side of the street completely oblivious to the whirlwind happening in his world across from her. It was just a passing moment, but it brought back years of grief and humiliation. Hurtful words and painful visions flashed through his mind, bringing desperately buried memories to life like demons rising from hell. He could feel the all too familiar dark depression creep back over him like the lid to a coffin. "Dammit" he muttered under his breath. Watching her until she disappeared into a sea of strangers, he wondered what on earth he would have done had she seen him there as well. The world suddenly seemed small and claustrophobic. His proud but wounded mind seemed to whimper and it was all he could do not to run.

A trigger is something that sparks a memory of an unhealed part of our life. When we experience hurt or shock, we tend to associate the experience with certain things and attach extra meaning to them. This attachment is what links the trigger, and us, to the unhealed situation. The trigger might be a song, a phrase, a place, a person, a smell, an article of clothing, or a kind of food. Being shocked back into a painful part of your life through an associated item is something we all experience at some point.

Archangel Jeremiel is the angel of life review. He helps us to review our lives so that we can heal past hurts that have now become triggers. He understands that the past is one of the greatest pain points of our lives, and so he teaches us how to extract the lessons we need so that we can leave the rest behind. He is not to be confused with Archangel Azrael, who helps us to grieve what has been lost. Archangel Jeremiel helps us to uncover the lessons from our past so that we can utilize them in our present day. He teaches us that triggers are simply areas of our lives we need to take a closer look at, and heal. In this, he helps us understand the difference between knowledge and wisdom, and helps us master the latter. He tells us that while knowledge can be found in books, wisdom only comes from learning from our past and putting those lessons into action.

Whenever we have an unhealed part of our past that has turned into a trigger, we tend to avoid the trigger at all cost. For example: "My mother used to punish me by hitting me and putting soap in my mouth, and I never buy that soap now." The unhealed event is the little child who was being abused, but the trigger or point of avoidance is what we have associated with the event- the soap. Was the soap the abuser? Is the soap to blame? No. It is the trigger. It's just soap. What is really being avoided here is the abuse. Another popular example that I hear is "I can't listen to that song, it brings back too many memories." The pain point isn't really the song, but all of the memories that the song brings. So, instead of dealing with the memories, we stay away from the trigger, thinking that by avoiding the association, we will be okay. But if you really want to be successful and happy, you're going to have to be willing to heal what the trigger is bringing up for you. When we don't deal with our past hurts, we walk around with so many triggers that the people around us have to walk on eggshells to keep from setting one of them off. Not only that, but anything we do not face, we tend to project onto other people because their actions become triggers for us. Life gets really claustrophobic, dense, and hard when this happens. Thank goodness we have the example of Archangel Jeremiel who fearlessly looks into the past to heal the pain points and release all triggers so that we can be free and liberated from so much suffering.

In order to objectively review yourself, you must be willing to understand that you are not your past. You must be willing to understand that the situations and patterns and people in your life created your experiences; they didn't create you. Looking at your past from a detached point of view will help you to recognize why you hold on and repeat self-destructive behaviors. Understanding creates awareness; awareness helps you break the cycles.

Easier said than done, right? I know that it's incredibly hard to let go of pain. If you've held onto it for a long time, it feels like an old friend. It feels justified and that it would be sacrilegious to let it go. But why allow your life to be defined by your pain? It's not healthy, it adds to your stress, it hurts your ability to focus, study and work, and it impacts every other relationship you have- even the ones not directly affected by the hurt. Every day you choose to hold on to the pain is another day everybody around you has to live with that decision. And feel its consequences.

Archangel Jeremiel helps us to feel empowered by showing us the gift within every hardship. He also teaches that the remedy for humiliation is to learn humility. Like the story above, what kinds of humiliation, dread, and embarrassing situations are you still suffering from? Would learning humility help? You're just learning, you're just growing, and you're just trying things and growing. *If you're not making mistakes, you're not trying*. Due to your past hurts, you may be afraid to take action. However, sitting around letting yourself be tormented by your failures and letting that prevent you from acting is the surest way to fail. Don't be afraid of mistakes. Mistakes are proof that you're out there being a fearless badass. And that is the essence of Archangel Jeremiel. He will help you move out of the past and become reborn for a different, brighter future.

If Archangel Jeremiel were a human, he would be a counselor. And while compassion and understanding would exude from his every pore, I believe he would also show a lot of toughness in his counseling. Archangel Jeremiel would feel passionate about helping you to overcome your hardships. He would be a strong advocate for your own personal "JUST GET OVER IT" movement while still taking a constructive and compassionate approach to accomplishing this. He would help you learn how to laugh at your mistakes and let yourself off the hook so that you can move on. He would be an author of self help books, and would frequently be interviewed as the "just get over it" doctor.

Archangel Jeremiel would most likely be the type of man who had several streams of income. His vivacious energy would allow him to try and fail several times as an entrepreneur until he finally became successful at several different things. He would also be athletic and involved with sports for the same reasons. He would be motivated by failure until he became successful at anything he put his mind to. He would be an example of how perseverance, forgiveness of the past, and the will to move on with lessons in tact creates massive success.

Archangel Jeremiel would most likely live near mountains where he could ski, bike, hike, and go camping. He might even be involved in extreme sports like ice climbing, skydiving, and rafting. He would be active, and would perfect each endeavor he participated in by practicing being in the present moment with each task. Dressed casually, you would be able to spot his athletic build along with a broad smile and understanding eyes. You would instantly feel as though you could confide in this strong motivator, knowing that he could help you to find a way to conquer the pain of your past. At the end of the day, Archangel Jeremiel would be stretching his sore muscles from practicing some sort of physical activity and reviewing his latest business plan. He would be 'taking stalk of the day', and letting go of any disappointment, worries, and cares so that he could be renewed for the next day of counseling, playing, and living completely in the moment.

How You Can Be Like Archangel Jeremiel

Your willingness to review your past with much humility, compassion, and understanding is key to being like this powerful being. If you want to be like Archangel Jeremiel, be willing to put away the beat up stick and objectively look at your past with fresh non judging eyes.

There may also be a time when you have to deal with someone else's past. No one leaves this earth without making seeming mistakes, learning lessons, and going through something that helps them to grow. We all take a turn playing the bad guy, the martyr, the victim, or the hero. It is important to not only let go of your past, but the past of others-especially if you can see that they have learned and grown from their past mistakes. I do understand that learning people's pasts can help you to know them better in the present, however, take people's pasts with a grain of salt. Give everyone a fresh now start when you meet them. You certainly wouldn't want to be judged by the worst part of your past, right?

"A man must be big enough to admit his mistakes, smart enough to profit from them, and strong enough to correct them."-John C. Maxwell

The Mind State

Introspection: Recognize that feeling irritated or triggered by something is like an invitation from your soul to see beyond the trigger and do some major inner healing. Whenever you are feeling triggered by anything, know that it is time for some introspection. Just like managers will give employee reviews, it is a good idea to give yourself a life review every so often to gauge your progress and make necessary changes. This self review should be a gentle and honest opportunity to recuperate from life's challenges, to reflect on the way ahead, strengthen yourself and prepare for the next phase of life. During times of introspection, you can become aware of your gifts, your inner reserve, and your wisdom. It is a time of healing.

Release: Very often we find ourselves holding on to the past in order to protect ourselves from making the same mistake in the future. However, the opposite usually ends up happening. You can create the same mistakes over and over when you are still linked to the pain of your past. If you find yourself in the same types of dramas, issues, and problems, it is usually due to unresolved issues that you have yet to release and let go of and the need to hold on to the pain thinking that somehow you are protecting yourself by doing so. After introspection, it is necessary to clean up the past and move on with greater wisdom and lessons learned. You are in fact safer once you release the pain of your past and less prone to repeating the same lessons once they are fully accepted and learned.

The Work

It takes a tremendous amount of consistent discipline and hard work to learn how to stay present. Our minds are often like unruly, undomesticated animals that have to be trained to sit and stay. This is why we call meditation a "practice." Just as you would have to practice each command with a new puppy in order to train it, you must spend the time practicing and training yourself to obey and sit still. Just like having an out of control dog in your house creates chaos and havoc, so does living with an out of control mind.

The work requires you to create time to practice being present. You can do this by setting an alarm on your phone to go off every hour, and when it does just stop whatever you are doing, take in a deep breath, and focus on your immediate surroundings, how your body feels, and how you would like to feel. You can also create longer periods of time where you can either go for a walk or sit and breathe and just practice bringing your wild mind back to center and into your present moment. When we practice being present, we become fully aware of our current surroundings and what we are really doing. We turn off auto-pilot and fill our actions with purpose and intent. It is in this zone we are our most powerful and most productive.

Another part of the work involves writing down your triggers. What do you purposely avoid because it brings up pain from your past? By acknowledging and seeing what triggers your pain, you are being brave enough to begin a process to healing them. After you admit your triggers, you can then begin to detach them from the real pain. An example of this would be, "The smell of cigars reminds me of my abusive step father, but it's not really the smell that is hurting me. Cigar smoke is just cigar smoke. My real issue is my step father. Therefore, I can let my feelings towards the smell of cigars go and release my unhealthy attachment to it. In fact, when I do not associate cigar smoke to my step father, I rather like it!" Another would be, "that song brings back painful memories because it was played at my wedding and now I'm getting a divorce. However, the song is not my pain point. The divorce is. I can let this song be its beautiful song and appreciate the artist and music knowing that I'm really just avoiding the pain of my divorce. When I turn the song off, the pain will still be there until I heal it. And when I really think about it and separate it from my pain, it's a great song."

It feels good to look at your triggers as separate from your pain. Letting go of your attachment to so many things brings you more freedom and liberation. You won't walk around avoiding so much. You are free to build a new experience with each trigger.

Once you've acknowledged your triggers and begin the process to healing them, take a look into your past for the good things. Write down every big and small success you've achieved. This may include lessons you've learned from seeming mistakes along with accomplishments you're proud of. Take time to celebrate how far you have come. Do something to celebrate by taking yourself out for a lovely dinner or on a nice trip. Buy yourself something to represent your level of achievement. I actually printed out a fake Certificate of Achievement after I went through a really hard time in my life. It was my "Badass Award" and I displayed it proudly! Appreciating yourself will give you confidence and energy to continue moving forward! I once heard that we are not born with self esteem, but that we cultivate it by acknowledging what we overcome. Celebrate your successes and you'll not only improve yourself perception and esteem, but you'll finally get the acknowledgement you deserve!

Real Life

There are so many helpful lessons and wisdom that can be acquired by glancing into our past. While we don't want to dwell on regrets or remorse, history can teach us a lot about where we are going. One of the best examples of this is the current popular saying, "Keep Calm and Carry On." While this saying has been reproduced and made into many fun memes and sayings, there is a very endearing historic story behind it.

In the spring of 1939 during the buildup to war with Germany, the British government began a series of propaganda posters with intentions to create calmness in the midst of pending fear and crisis. They used the crown of King George VI and a simple color and font scheme to make them uniform in appearance. The first poster read, "Your Courage, Your Cheerfulness, Your Resolution Will Bring Us Victory." The second poster read, "Freedom is In Peril, Defend it With All Your Might." The third poster simply read, "Keep Calm and Carry On." The first two posters were displayed everywhere in shop windows and street corners. However, the third was not ever released, even though it was printed over 2.5 million times. A copy of it was found 50 years later inside an old second hand book shop called Barter Books in the north east corner of England. The bookshop owners loved the print and so they hung it up. It was so popular with the customers, that they found the first two posters and began selling copies of all three. It is so interesting to me how a phrase from decades ago would be so appealing to our current society. Its design is simple, timeless, and recognized worldwide. It is as though a beautiful whisper from history has finally been heard and understood. And perhaps like many things from our past that go unnoticed until the perfect time, the whisper wasn't supposed to be heard until now. After all, I believe now more than ever the entire world deserves the comfort that the phrase intended. "Keep Calm and Carry On."

This next story has always made an impact on my clients when I have told it to them, and really sets the tone for how balancing learning from our past while staying present is so important.

"Two monks were on a pilgrimage. One day, they came to a deep river. At the edge of the river, a young woman sat weeping because she was afraid to cross the river without help. She begged the two monks to help her. The younger monk turned his back. The members of their order were forbidden to touch a woman.

But the older monk picked up the woman without a word and carried her across the river. He put her down on the far side and continued his journey. The younger monk came after him, scolding him and berating him for breaking his vows. He went on this way for a long time.

Finally, at the end of the day the older monk turned to the younger one. 'I only carried her across the river. You have been carrying her all day.'"

Archangel Jeremiel's Message To The Modern World: *"Imagine how fun life could be if you didn't have so many triggers. If people, songs, things, situations from your past arose and you didn't have to relive all of the emotional pain that your memories cause you to have. You could enjoy things, you could actually get to know people and offer them more of yourself. You would be liberated from the heaviness that comes from shying away from certain things that you have given power to hurt you. Memories bring the painful situation into your present moment, and while the actual event is over, your body and mind experience it over and over again through the memories. The trick is to learn how to get quiet. The undisciplined part of your mind will run the painful memory over and over like a tired record player until you can get quiet and learn how to just observe how your mind does this. Do not fight your mind, just simply* *watch as it relates to triggers. When you separate yourself from your wounded mind, you will begin to detach your emotional reaction to what is being replayed. You are not your mind; you are watching it, receiving it, aware of it. Detaching from your mind will allow you to become more present and begin to review the painful past with the intent to find the gift. Even the most horrendous pasts hold within them a gift to make you greater. Perhaps it is the gift of forgiveness, mercy, self love and acceptance. Perhaps it is the gift of strength, wisdom, or an idea to help someone else or to solve a problem. Perhaps the gift is in the healing of it, simply learning how to let go and free yourself. Once you find your gift, you will be free of the triggers that were associated with the pain and life can begin anew."*

Questions To Consider: Is it time for a little life review? What are you willing to learn from your past so that you don't repeat the same mistakes? What are you willing to learn from your past that works that you can implement today? Are you tired of having so many triggers to your past? What are the gifts that your past has for you? These are things to think about if you want to be like the merciful, forgiving, and understanding Archangel Jeremiel.

Chapter 7

Archangel Jophiel- The Celebrity

Put Your Best Self Out There

There is an air of anticipation in the woods today. The excitement is building knowing the procession is arriving. Animals and creatures of all types sniff the air and gather together for the big event. At the first sound of faraway bells, the air becomes electric with exhilaration and it seems as though everything has taken a deep gasp as the first fairy lights appear off in the distance, coming closer. As the front of the parade arrives, the trees finally seem to settle with enjoyment, and all of the animals begin to dance around merrily. Birds begin to sing and fly about in rehearsed patterns making the whole scene look alive and magical. The procession has arrived! It is here! The music made from odd handmade instruments wafts through the air. Everything is bright, jubilant, and jovial. As the fairy procession continues through this place, you can see magnificent little beings dancing in and around beautiful carriages made out of dainty shoes, old fashioned toy cars, boats and other vintage items. The air is filled with glittery paper snowflakes, and airplanes. You are surrounded by things only your childhood imagination could possibly dream. All of the sudden, what is this? The one and only fairy queen atop a magnificent float made from flowers and leaves. The drums are playing loudly and the whole forest is dancing to the rhythm in synchronistic joy. She is tall, lovely, and glowing with radiant joy. Her gaze stops as she sees you and she motions for her float to cease as she gracefully descends to where you are standing. You watch her in absolute awe. The music has shifted to a slower, sweet lullaby-like melody, it seems familiar but you are too busy focusing on how to present yourself to the royal beauty. From

behind her meticulously sewn skirts, she magically retrieves a
stunning pearl handled mirror. She points it to you and you
do as she motions and peer into it. You vaguely hear the
music and celebration now as your eyes find themselves in the
mirror. Your eyes are almost the only thing you recognize, as
your reflection is showing you a perfect, radiant, healed,
exquisite version of you. Her voice sounds like wind chimes as
she simply tells you, "This is who you truly are. This is who
you are and who you were before the world told you who to
be." This truth seems to fit inside of you like some sort of
missing puzzle piece. You take one last astonished look at
yourself before the mirror is gone and she has flitted back
atop her float. She signals for the music to pick up again and
begins waving at all of her lovely forest creatures. The
procession moves forward, ever forward, with all of your
dreams, wishes, and truth with it. Will you join it?

Archangel Jophiel is exactly how her name sounds- jovial. She is the Archangel of beauty as her name means "Beauty of God." She helps uplift you by helping you to beautify your thoughts. She helps you to see, appreciate, and manifest more beauty into your life. But most of all, she helps you to see the beauty within yourself!

The best way to describe Archangel Jophiel is by saying that she is the "BFF" everyone needs in their lives, inspiring us to take a vacation or relax when life gets ugly. She feels like a breath of fresh air, and inspires you to make your living area beautiful. She also recognizes the need for you to feel like you look good, and acknowledges that how you view yourself is exactly how you will present yourself to the world.

Years ago, I used to watch a show on TLC called "What Not To Wear." It proved to be controversial as many people who watched (and participated in) the show felt more comfortable looking a certain way on the pretense that they wanted people to treat them based on who they were on the inside- not how they appeared. What I believe most people found once they put away their stubborn views, was that when they allowed their inner radiance to be seen on the outside, they finally felt integrated with whom they truly were on the inside. You know what it feels like to put on something that you feel really proud and comfortable in. You know what a really nice pair of shoes can do for you. Ladies, when your make-up lets your eyes sparkle and your lips shine; you know how that you come off more confidant. Guys, when you look in the mirror and see you wearing something that exudes respect, strength, and confidence, you know you walk with a more assured stride. And if you do not know what any of that feels like, go out and try it out! Taking the time to put your best self out there is worth it! You never know when opportunity will strike and when you will need to be on point, looking the part, and ready for success!

If Archangel Jophiel were human, I believe she'd be a celebrity. Absolutely natural in the limelight, wearing the latest trend and pulling it off like a boss! She would revel in spa dates, exotic vacations, and having her picture taken would never be a nuisance. She would surround herself with other fun-loving, genuine, and optimistic people. Following her on social media would be a positive, fabulous, fun breath of fresh air with every post. She would be a natural actress, able to flit in and out of roles and wardrobes. Even on her off days, she would sport cute pink sweats while eating the highest quality of chocolate and admiring her new Chanel bag. Of course none of this would make her shallow, don't even think that about this powerful little beauty! Archangel Jophiel would understand that luxuries are our birthright, and that when we open ourselves to having it all, it doesn't change us unless we have judgments about being wealthy and glamorous. She would understand that none of that makes her who she is, only that she deserves to be adored, admired, and treated well by the world. Not only that, but she would also know that she deserved the very best! By working hard to get what she wanted, she would revel in the lush treats, shiny awards, sparkling jewelry, and fabulous shoes! All of those things to her would represent her dedication to herself and show her earned hard work. Her message would always be to "go ahead, let yourself have it all! Really, it's okay to have beautiful things and to feel handsome, successful, sexy, powerful, and prestigious!" Her charities would be to provide upscale clothing for poor single mothers who are looking to get a higher paying job. In this way, she would be able to honor her code of "The world treats you how you look," by giving women a chance to feel beautiful and go for better opportunities. She would also feel passionate about clothing the entire world, and you may see her on commercials that are asking for clothing and advocate donations for third world countries.

In her spare time, Archangel Jophiel would study art and theater and she would appreciate the talent and effort it takes to create a masterpiece. She would also love spending time in beautiful nature, surrounded by fields of flowers, or taking in a gorgeous sunset. Picturesque picnics adorned with a classic wicker basket, overly large comfy blanket, bohemian pillows, fancy wine and fresh organic grapes with her girlfriends would tickle her pink! She would live in Hollywood and you'd see her in her Bentley on her way to somewhere beautiful and glamorous. People may be jealous, or judge her, but none of that would even matter to her world of lovely, wonderful, happy things.

How You Can Be Like Archangel Jophiel

In what area of your life do you need more beauty, fun, and lavish abundance? We discussed how patience can make you pretty in Archangel Haniel's section, however there are more virtues that you can practice that will help you beautify yourself, relationships, surroundings, and image. Attributes such as compassion, understanding, humor, assertiveness, clarity, optimism, playful, charitable, giving, and being thoughtful. What other attributes make someone beam with beauty? Archangel Jophiel would be watching people and deciding what she thinks makes them beautiful, and she would be taking action steps to become more like them. You can do that too if you want to be like her.

When do you feel most ugly or undesirable? If you want to be like Archangel Jophiel and radiate joy everywhere you go, you must be willing to take stock, and look deep within for the areas, ideas, thoughts, and actions that are making you feel unattractive. Perhaps you are feeling vengeful over something someone did or maybe you feel jealous and insecure. Maybe you are taking your stress out on the people closest to you. These are all things that when left unchecked, can lead to a lot of ugliness in your life. You absolutely deserve to live lush! You deserve the finest that life has to offer! Begin to beautify your life by beautifying yourself!

"Always Do Your Best. Your best is going to change from moment to moment; it will be different when you are healthy as opposed to sick. Under any circumstance, simply do your best, and you will avoid self-judgment, self-abuse and regret."-Don Miguel Ruiz

The Mind State

Shine: The fear of outshining others is sometimes enough to keep us from being radiantly bold and beautiful. It is a fear that tells us to turn down our genius and abilities so that others do not feel threatened by it. If you are not as successful as you would like to be, ask yourself if it is because you are afraid of outshining someone you believe deserves it more than you. You may also wonder if you will be alone in your success. Will you be separated from the pack if you allow yourself to be the radiant, smart, talented person you know you really are? Worries like these will keep you from shining as brightly as you can. However, the truth is that the people who stand with you at your worst, will most likely be the same ones who will stand with you at your best. Those who feel threatened by your success aren't supposed to be in your life. Sometimes we meet people whose roles are to help us when we are at our lowest points and when we get back onto our feet, they seem to drift away. That's okay, let them go. If the relationship is supposed to last through your journey, it will. Whatever you do, don't shrink or be small on the account of others. Your success has the potential to inspire and bless everyone around you, so go ahead and put your best self out there!

Beautify your mind: Jophiel is the Archangel of beauty and joy. She can be a shining example of how to keep your mind from going dark and dismal when things are going great for you. You know the scenario, you feel great and energized by life, possibilities are endless, things are great and then it happens. Your mind, like a frightened prisoner begins to flood you with doubts, worries, fears, and even visions of irrational outcomes. You find yourself straying from your bright happy path and into a dark scary forest full of twisty and shady uncertainties.

The first step here is to recognize what your mind is doing. Negative thoughts are normal- everyone has them. Shakespeare wrote, "Our doubts are traitors and make us lose the good we oft might win, by fearing to attempt." Understand that there is a part of your mind that takes its job to sabotage you very seriously. Its whole purpose is to dull your sparkle in order to keep you "safe." If you can see this mind trick for what it is, it will be easy to allow yourself to brush away the cobwebs, put your hand up to the inner nay saying, and find your happy path again.

The outer world is a reflection of your inner world, so focus on the beauty within yourself; your good qualities, your kindness, and what you are good at. Everyone has beauty in their soul, so find it in others too! Remind people of their best qualities and spread beauty everywhere you go. The more you tune into the incredible wonder and beauty within yourself and others, you will begin to radiate. Seeing and radiating beauty will have you standing out in the crowd, and others will be touched by it!

Joy: Joy springs from your sense of connection to your creator, who is the source of joy. Whenever you feel that connection, you will feel illuminated with joy. Then, life will become a celebration! Life is meant to be fun and joyous. So, stay connected to the source of joy and you will become aware of the wonder, delight, and celebration that is meant for you. Joy is a key to enlightenment; allow it into your life daily by pursuing your passions, playing, and remembering to find things to laugh about.

The Work

You know that really dumpy, frumpy, sad excuse for an article of clothing you own? The one you justify keeping because it's your "sad day sweatshirt," or "most comfy pj's" or your "period panties" or "my smelly high school team jersey" or "my one day I'm going to need this because I'll be painting or camping or shoveling horse crap..."? Get. Rid. Of. It. And while you're at it, go through your closet one article of clothing at a time and ask yourself as you really look at it, "does this piece of clothing make me feel happy and successful?" If the answer is no, GET. RID. OF. IT! If you wouldn't be caught dead in something, why are you holding it hostage in your closet? And regarding clothing you don't fit into, GET. RID. OF. IT! What kind of guilt message are you sending yourself each time you see that swimsuit you can fit into anymore? It's presence in your closet is not going to magically shred your body to fit into it again. Treat yourself to a brand new one that you feel sexy in and won't taunt you. Beautify your wardrobe and if you have no idea where to start, consider hiring an expert or talking to someone you think looks great. Or just simply get out there, do the work, and try stuff on!

After you go through your clothing, look through your house. Pretend you are moving into a smaller place and you have to get rid of a fourth of everything you own. If you come across something you haven't used in a year or longer, Get. Rid. Of. It. Focus on beautifying your home and surroundings by decluttering and then adding things you love. Does your home reflect who you truly are as a person? Does it speak of your potential, goals, and success? Ask yourself, "If I did not know myself, what would I think about the person living here?" Create the type of living space you truly want to live in-one that supports your goals and dreams.

Recently, I learned a deeper definition of what "abundance" means. Abundance isn't necessarily having a lot of things, but loving every single thing you own. When you walk through your home, office, garage, and closet and you love every single thing in it, you feel abundant- no matter how many things you actually have. Abundance is more about quality than quantity. When you love everything you own, you will feel as though you have enough. When you don't like everything you own, you feel lack because you will want more. So, as you are letting things go, keep in mind that you are really increasing the feelings of abundance by creating a situation where you don't necessarily have a lot of things that you "kind of" like, but that you only have things that you truly love. Create a life where you literally and absolutely love each piece of clothing, each pair of shoes, every dish in your cupboards, and every tool in your shed. Let the things you're not so crazy about go, and make room for true abundance. Abundance and beauty go hand in hand. When you love everything you own, you will see beauty all around!

Real Life

I was raised by parents who valued their appearance. My father wore nice suits to work every day, and my mother always looked stunning when we went out for dinner or to Sunday church. Most of all, I was taught by my parents that if you looked important you would be treated as such. I remember as a little girl watching my father shave, tie his tie, and fasten his cuff links. He would carry his attaché case in the same hand that his nice watch peeked out from under his tailored sleeve. Everyone who worked in his offices seemed to respect his authority because he wore it well. My dad looked classy, assertive, and important- and because of that he was treated accordingly. What I knew about my dad however, was that he was really a Wyoming boy at heart. I knew he was happiest when he was getting his hands dirty fishing along the Snake River, hiking, or tending his garden. Outside of his office uniform, I saw him drop popcorn on his old sweatshirt as we played video games and indulge in fudge brownie ice cream as a midnight snack. But when it came to the way he wanted to be treated by the world, it seems as though my dad understood that he had to look the part.

How my upbringing has translated to my adult life is that I understand the value of looking professional if I want to be taken seriously. This belief was validated years ago during the first semester of college in a business class. I remember as I looked around the classroom, I shifted uncomfortably in my seat realizing once again that I must have overdressed. This was college, right? It seemed as though every student showed up in sweats, flannels, and one person was actually wearing slippers. I acknowledged it was an early class but come on.

As I sat there in my college class considering what it would feel like to show up the next day in my lounge clothing, the professor introduced us to a local CEO who was looking for interns for the summer. Now, I'll be the first to admit I was definitely not the smartest person in the class. We all looked over at the boy who was an obvious 'A' student only to catch him looking down at his silly worn plaid sweatpants. He was in no shape to shake the hand of the president of any company. I took a deep breath, smoothed down my skirt and stood up. The professor promptly introduced me to the CEO and I got the opportunity on the spot!

After class, Mr. Straight 'A' attempted to insult me by calling it a lucky chance. This single experience taught me that luck is simply opportunity meeting preparation. When you are dressed and ready for the opportunities you want, you deserve the success!

Archangel Jophiel's Message To The Modern World: *"The most important thing you can do is to beautify your thoughts. With lovely thoughts, one can create lovely words. Your actions will reflect the loveliness in your mind, and people will be drawn to you. When ugly or unpleasant thoughts arise, simply flush them out by saying a positive affirmation such as, "Everything will be okay. I love and accept myself, what I do, and who I am, even in the midst of this." The way your life looks, the way your body looks, the way your house looks, the way your income looks, the way your partner looks, the way your children look, the way your car looks, the way your health looks, the way your world looks is a direct result of your thoughts. Beautify your mind- sweep away the cobwebs, dirt from your past, other people's grime, and organize your inner self. This one thing can change everything drastically into the stunning lush life you are meant to live. Think beautiful- be beautiful!"*

Questions To Consider: Are you willing to weed out the ugly to make room for more beautiful things in your life? Do you value yourself enough to make YOU a priority and put your best self out there? Do you shy away from riches or do you hoard them all to yourself? Do you believe you can be abundantly successful and humble? Is it possible for you to have everything you want despite what others may think of you? These are things you may want to ask yourself if you want to be like the beautiful, outgoing, shining star, Archangel Jophiel.

Chapter 8

Archangel Metatron- The Superhero

Wake Up, Kick Ass, Repeat

He sits, his eyes watchful and alert. Seeing things he wishes he could fix, watching the people he wants to save. He looks like anybody else, sitting there on the park bench seeming to enjoy the sun while reading a paper. Passersby don't seem to notice him, but he notices them. He sees the stress on the man as he rushes to his job. He sees the sleepless night on the face of the teen who skates by to his next drug deal. He watches the mother who desperately needs a break as she pushes her baby in the stroller. They are all in their own little worlds, not noticing each other, or much of what goes on around them. They each have needs, unfulfilled desires, pain, hopelessness. Just then, a sound shatters the air like glass, no, like bells. Everyone perks up to focus on the giggling child as he watches his grandfather make funny faces from behind his hands. The giggling turns into side splitting laughter and the rosy cheeked child falls down, losing himself in the moment of pure joy. And just like that, the contagious laughter spreads smiles among the onlookers. The man rushing to work hesitates as his entire thought process is interrupted by loving memories of his own children at home. The teen picks up his skateboard and walks slower wondering if he should stop all this madness. The mother stops, lifts the blanket from her sleeping child and lovingly gazes upon her sweet angelic face, her gratitude pushing away the tiredness and turning it into fuel to continue. The laughing child is memorized by his grandfathers antics, completely lost in his own happiness, however, that happiness is strong enough to break through everyone's walls and negativity. The watchful man on the bench smiles to himself. Once again, love and joy reigns supreme, and all is restored in the world once more. These people don't need a savior, he concludes to himself. Given the right tools, they are perfectly capable of saving themselves. And with that he leaves the area, feeling surer of the human race more than ever.

To be completely honest, Archangel Metatron was the hardest Archangel to try and put a label onto. I mean, just look at his name-Metatron. He sounds more like a transformer than an Archangel. He is bigger than any single section I could possibly write in a book and he has a vast history in and out of religious lore and scripture. You can begin to see this in the fact that among the 15 Archangels, both Metatron and Sandalphon (of whom you'll read about later) are the only ones whose name do not end in "el". That is because it is said that "el" stands for Elohim, the name of God. Archangels Metatron and Sandalphon are believed to have been human before ascending into the Archangel realm. Archangel Metatron is believed to have been the prophet Enoch- scribe and author of The Book of Enoch. He is known for creating and using the Metatron Cube, which is a sacred geometrical shape also called a Merkaba. This shape has been discussed by many spiritual theorists to possibly be the original tree of life, and you can see variations of it within the Kabala, and ancient Jewish texts.

As an author, scribe, and with his sacred geometry, Archangel Metatron is a teacher of esoteric knowledge. However, there is another side to this Archangel that I feel more compelled to write about. Archangel Metatron takes a special interest in highly sensitive young people who are misunderstood or even medicated because their spiritual gifts make them socially awkward. This includes children diagnosed with ADD, ADHD, and the ranges of autism and Asperger's Syndrome. Because this is a controversial subject, and the fact that I don't want to get too much into it, I will simply say that while there are real diagnosis, people who really suffer from neurotransmitter disorders and Autism, there is also the fact that we are over-diagnosing and overlooking children who are extremely gifted, learn in different capacities, and are evolving away from our current educational structure. We seem to think that if a child cannot sit still and do nothing but repetitive worksheets all day for 6 hours, that there is something neurologically wrong with them. Humans were not created to live that way. Humans were not made to run like machines, yet when we fail to do so at a young age, we are "corrected with harsh chemical medications. None of that makes any sense to the 15, especially the powerful and mighty Archangel Metatron, who works tirelessly with children, doctors, teachers, and parents. He wants to help us to understand that humans are meant to operate freely, and to help us find more effective ways to educate children.

It is a fact that when humans are given enough rest, enjoyment, relaxation, healthy foods, and motivation, that we can accomplish any task that is asked of us. However, when we live stressed out, tired, overworked, underappreciated, underpaid, unhealthy lives, our productivity decreases drastically. We become like zombies and we search for things to numb out the pain of not being allowed to live like a natural human being. Higher conscious schools and corporations understand this now, and instead of offering medication and caffeine to their students and employees, they are offering more breaks, fun, and a healthier relaxed environment. They are seeing in both schools and businesses that tasks can be done in shorter amounts of time, with less mistakes and more productivity when the stress of their employees and students is decreased. Some companies are even considering shortening the workweek to fit what their employees actually get accomplished so that there isn't so much time waiting on the clock. It is easier to prioritize and get things done if you know you can leave when you are finished, rather than having to stretch out your time until the bell rings or the whistle blows.

Archangel Metatron knows that the best way to save anyone is to help them save themselves. That is why being patient, understanding people's needs, and believing in them more than they believe in themselves is so important to him. I've labeled him a superhero, but not because we are weak and need one. Rather because when we strive to be like him, to be our best, and stand up for what we believe in, we become our own superheroes. Archangel Metatron is one of the strongest Archangels in the realm; he has a no tolerance for bullshit attitude and as you'll see in the next section, his presence with the mighty warrior Archangel Michael forms an unstoppable duo. Together they are here to help us to save ourselves. They do this by encouraging us to quit being so helpless and actually muster up the courage to create radical changes.

The dysfunctions within our educational system-from the way education is actually presented to our children to the fact that only the wealthy are able to get quality from it by paying for better schools-is a subject that rings close to Archangel Metatron's heart, and is something worth taking a stand on. And also, as you'll see in the real life story below, taking the issues into our own hands and recognizing that we are not victims to anything is necessary if you want to be like the powerful Archangels. There is more than one way to get educated, and more than one way to get what you want with anything if you're willing to be different than the rest.

As a human, Archangel Metatron would have the desire to expose what isn't working in our education systems while empowering those in positions of power to influence effective change. There would be no blame, shame, or judgment in his whistleblowing, as he would focus more on the issues, not the people- and more on solutions than the problems. He would be a motivational speaker, and with his laser sharp intent and focus, help people to take accountability over their own lives to make radical corrections in the world. He would feel passionate about helping children, acknowledging their roles in the future of our planet. He would have a boisterous sense of humor, almost comedic in the way he exposed the things we put up with, sweep under the rug, and ignore. He would help us to laugh at some of our crazy traditions, and let go of systems that do not work.

Archangel Metatron would most likely live in New Zealand or Australia and appreciate the rough and tough "get 'er done" outback mentality. However, he wouldn't be home much, as traveling and speaking to corporations, educational departments, medical conferences, and even the United Nations would be the norm in his life. He would also be a popular speaker at universities and schools around the world. Even though he would prove to be extremely upfront, honest, and often controversial, the majority would salute his ability to create solutions and offer empowerment and motivation. He would visit places where children need help such as orphanages, shelters, and third world countries. In his spare time, Archangel Metatron would enjoy sightseeing and visiting historic places and reading historical books. He would also enjoy a good laugh telling jokes around a campfire, or watching a funny movie. Of course, his big strong belly laugh would be contagious and anyone would love to be around this powerful man. At the end of the day, he would probably be reviewing his next speech, editing his latest article, answering e-mails, and anticipating the next day where he would wake up, kick ass, and repeat!

How You Can Be Like Archangel Metatron

You can be like Archangel Metatron by being willing to authentically look at your world and ask yourself what needs to change. Ask yourself what you are sweeping under the rug and what little nuisances are bugging you in the back of your mind. A true superhero looks at themselves first. Where do you feel weak and helpless? Start there. Once on the path to self development, you will begin to learn through your own experiences how to help others. This could look many different ways for each of us. You may wish to better yourself in order to make more money to gain the ability to help others. You may be inspired to lose excess weight so that you can begin to inspire and show others a healthier way to live. Whatever changes you decide to make are ones you feel the whole world needs to make. In the wise advice of Gandhi, a real superhero must be the change they wish to see in the world.

Being a superhero doesn't mean you start doing things for others that they would be better off doing themselves. It means that you are more committed to helping them feel empowered to save themselves, rather than actually saving them. It means that you may push or nudge someone a little. It means you may raise the bar for them. It means that instead of saving someone from their burning tower, you send them clear instructions, tools, show them, and then cheer them on as they save themselves. You never want to be someone's sole reason for bettering themselves- you want them to say they did it because of your example. The truth is, once you save someone, you're always going to have to be saving them because they never learned how to do it themselves. You will feel much better about being an example, rather than taking on the responsibility of "fixing" or saving someone. And remember, not everyone wants to change. A true superhero honors everyone's path, even if it is hard to watch them walk it.

"Personal transformation can and does have global effects. As we go, so goes the world, for the world is us. The revolution that will save the world is ultimately a personal one."-Marianne Williamson

The Mind State

Aspiration: It's time to set your sights higher. If you are settling for the mediocre, aim higher! Stretch yourself, raise your bar, go after something more. Inside of you is a voice that wants to enable you to aspire to greater heights. The only way you're going to reach your dreams, is to expand out of your comfort zone. Right now, commit to never settle for less than your incredible spirit can achieve and deserves.

Positivity: When you are positive, you radiate a high vibration that is undeniably attractive to other positive people, situations, and experiences. Your positivity is contagious and will make everyone and everything around you better. Choose your thoughts and attitudes so that they are focused on love, abundance, and success. People might challenge your optimistic approach to everything, but that is just because they are focused on fear, lack, and failure. Understand them, forgive them, shake off their response to you, and move on. This one change of mind state can greatly affect your entire life and all of your outcomes.

Accountability: How you do one thing is how you do all things. We like to pretend that our lives are compartmentalized, and that if we are unhappy in one area it won't affect other areas. Or if we are lazy in one area that we won't be lazy in other areas. But the truth is that unhappiness is unhappiness and laziness is laziness. Your life is one huge ecosystem, and when one area suffers it affects everything. You can't be one way in one aspect of your life, and not be that same way in other aspects. If you hate your job, that hate follows you home. If things aren't going well at home, it shows up in your work. If you overeat, over drink, or use drugs to avoid dealing with emotional issues, there's probably another part of your life where you are avoiding accountability too.

Being accountable means that you realize how much of an impact you make on the world. Your negativity affects other people. However, so does your joy. In fact, without your smile, this world wouldn't be the same. Your joy inspires people and your success shows others their potential. Whether you know it or not, whether you mean to or not, you broadcast a message to the world through your thoughts and actions. You are constantly teaching people ways to deal with stress and how to find happiness. This is because we all love watching each other. Perhaps this is why social media is so huge today. We love seeing how other people act and react to life. So if people are watching you, and we are, what message do you want to broadcast? How do you want to affect the world? You are powerful, and with power comes responsibility and accountability.

The Work

You may need to harness your own tendency to become "ADD" while prioritizing, reaching goals, and making positive changes. In this case, ADD can stand for Addictions, Drama, and Distractions. The closer you get to a goal, the more ADD you become. This is because your inner saboteur or inner villain is trying to keep you away from your success! Be your own superhero and put that inner villain away! Fight through the ADD and stay the course!

Make a list of things you love to do. Then make a list of things you actually do all day. How similar are those lists? Ask yourself honestly, "Who do I want to be, and what do I need to do in order to become that person? How can I become a better version of myself?"

Who are your heroes? What is it that you admire and what steps can you take to be like them? Everyone who wants to be successful needs a mentor, a way-shower, and someone to follow. It has been proven time and time again that success leads success. Here are a few real life examples of people who have created their own success with the experience of a mentor:

- Marc Andreessen (multi-millionaire founder of Mosaic and Netscape) mentor to Mark Zuckerberg (billionaire founder of Facebook)
- Warren Buffett (billionaire financier) mentor to Donald Graham (publisher, Washington Post) and Michael Lee-Chin (CEO, AIC Limited)
- Joe Weider mentor to Arnold Schwarzenegger
- Richard Burton mentor to Sir Anthony Hopkins

Aspiring to be like our mentors can help us to know what steps to take and decisions to make in order to have the kind of success we want. Doreen Virtue has been a mentor of mine for years. She is my hero, and the kind of life she lives today is one I aspire to. By having her in my life to look up to, I have been inspired and motivated to do things I otherwise wouldn't have.

Real Life

It was the third week of second grade for my oldest son when I began to notice it. He had always been such a cheerful, confident child, however as the days progressed it was as if a dark cloud had cast itself behind his eyes, and he seemed to be on edge, as if a storm was about to erupt in his life at any moment. He began saying things like, "I'm not very good at anything," and his energy levels were so low that he would come home from school and just lay in his bed. My growing concern lead me to go meet his new teacher and see what was going on at school, since nothing in his home life had changed.

The first thing I noticed as I walked into his teacher's classroom was the chaotic wall decorations and piles of books, papers, and mess everywhere. Her desk was unbelievable, stacked with a whirlwind of junk food, school supplies and assignments. I couldn't believe my son had been sitting in this room all day for three weeks! As I approached his teacher about my concerns, she was highly defensive. I assured her that in no way was I blaming her or the school for his sudden withdrawal, but I wished to discuss how to help him with her. She ranted for 15 minutes about how hard it is to be a teacher, that she had too many kids in her class, and that she felt overwhelmed. I felt bad for her and wondered what could be done to make this better. If she was uncomfortable in the class, I could imagine how all of the kids were feeling, not just my son. As I began doing research on my son's school district, it seemed as though all of their schools were understaffed. Further research suggested that it was because the pay was so low. I didn't blame any teacher for not wanting to teach in that district, overpopulated classrooms and no support! I felt completely helpless. Meanwhile, because I had "complained" to the teacher, the school decided to test my son to see if he had a learning disability without my knowledge. The next thing I knew, I was in a conference with his teacher and the principal being told four words that changed me as a parent forever. "Your son has ADD."

My first reaction was to laugh and reply very bluntly, "Your room has ADD." I made a point to look hard at the chaos that surrounded us. They were either not impressed by and/or didn't understand my accusation. As it was, my son did yoga with me almost every day, and I had taught him how to meditate. We spent time in the kitchen baking together, and we would hike every week. I would sit down and help him with his homework, and he was able to stay focused and on task with anything we did together. My son did not have attention deficit disorder. The system had ADD and the only way they saw to fix the problem was to medicate my son. My son did not need medication, he needed an environment in which he could grow, learn, and thrive in. I left the meeting dumbfounded. I had no idea what to do.

My second reaction didn't come until the next day and like the storm that had been brewing behind my sons eyes, I suddenly shifted from bewildered to angry and enraged. The entire educational system issue beat down on my heart like a sledge hammer. I'll be the first one to focus on how to manage a difficult situation and work things out among the people involved; however, this was not one of those situations. Within me emerged a mighty mother bear seething and wanting to protect my child from ridiculous accusations. I thought of the chaotic, loud classroom my little one was suffering in at that very moment. I wondered how the teacher was treating him after our meeting. I had suddenly had enough. I dropped everything and walked out of my work in the middle of the day, drove like a bat out of hell to the school, threw the front doors open, pounded my heels all the way down the hall to my son's classroom. When I opened the door, I didn't see him. His teacher, looking stunned by the intrusion pointed me to a room next door. When I opened up the room, I found my little boy alone with another teacher.

"What is going on here?" I demanded. The other teacher attempted to talk but I interrupted her. "Honey," I asked my son firmly, "What are you doing in here?" His answer shattered any hopes I had in working things out with the school. "I'm in this room because I'm dumb…." My eyes widened and my heart began to pound. Anything the teacher was attempting to say to me was not heard over the rushing sound within my ears and fire blazing in my eyes. I took my little boy by the hand and walked him over to his classroom. I told him to get his things and that we were leaving. His teacher looking defensive and offended came at me demanding to know what I was doing.

To this day the only thing I can credit my next actions to would be pure adrenaline and a deep seated instinct to protect my young. I completely freaked out. I began yelling at her about her room, the chaos, the mess, I remember yelling at her to leave and get a job somewhere where she could make a difference instead of ruining lives with her uneducated and non medical diagnosis. I just went crazy. I remember marching my son down to the principal's office and demanding that his records be removed and handed over to me immediately. Hearing my son tell me that he was dumb after just a few weeks of being in that school was all the evidence I needed to know that it wasn't the place for him and like the archangels who have zero tolerance for bullshit, I swooped in and saved us both from a lifetime of broken confidence and a label that didn't fit.

The next thing I remember was driving us over to a Barnes and Noble and we sat and drank hot chocolate while discussing what had happened. I wanted to make sure that I hadn't made things worse by freaking out in front of my son the way I did. I assured him that he wasn't dumb, but that we just needed to find the right school to support his genius. I told him how proud I was with everything he did at home, and that there was absolutely nothing wrong with him. My sons eyes were full of tears, and I worried until he finally said, "I've never seen you like that, mom. You did all that because you believe in me." He got it; hence the power of standing in as a superhero.

The next month was a tiring process as I searched out private schools, charter schools and other public schools looking for a solution. I even considered home schooling. It took some time and effort, and the process was uncomfortable, however I ended up finding the perfect fit for my son and in no time he was back to his confident happy self. Totally worth it!!!

What I learned from my experience is that 1.) Where you spend most of your day, affects who you are. Whether it is a classroom or an office, if you are treated as if you are less than who you are, eventually it will chip away at you and your life will inevitably go downhill. 2.) Human beings of all ages, in all positions, at all learning levels deserve to be treated with kindness and respect. So do their parents. 3.) Don't be afraid to look crazy and take massive action when numbers 1 and 2 aren't being honored. That's the only way changes happen, and trust me- change happens when enough people stand up as superheroes.

Archangel Metatron's Message To The Modern World: *"The world just needs more heroes and that's all there is to it. I'm recruiting, are you in? There is no limit to the amount of goodness you can put forth into this world. Big or small acts of kindness do the same thing- they give hope and* *empowerment to others. Whether you are holding the door open for an elderly person or going all in to support someone reach their ultimate goal, it's all the same. So, what big or small thing can you do right now to be a hero? Who needs your strength, your humor, a hand, your wisdom and example? There's no time to waste! Get out there and make things happen; First for yourself, and then for the people around you. Be big. Be badass. Be sober. And be the change. Power to the people! Out!"*

Questions To Consider: Are there children in your life who need your powerful voice to speak up for them? Are you saving people instead of empowering them? Have you become too serious about something? If so, what part of life can you laugh about? How can you find the humor in your situation? What is the most important change you can make right now? Do you believe in yourself enough to wake up and be awesome every single day? These are questions you will want to ask yourself if you want to be like the big hearted, big thinker, and big superhero, Archangel Metatron.

Chapter 9

Archangel Michael- The Leader

Be Brave

"When darkness falls
And surrounds you
When you fall down
When you're scared
And you're lost
Be brave
I'm coming to hold you now
When all your strength has gone
And you feel wrong
Like your life has slipped away
Follow me
You can follow me
And I will not desert you now
When your fire's died out
No one's there
They have left you for dead
Follow me
You can follow me
I will keep you safe
Follow me
You can follow me
I will protect you"
-Muse-Follow Me

　　Archangel Michael's name means "He who is like God." He is probably the most well known of all Archangels. He is mentioned in almost every religious text across the globe, and is prevalent in both old and new age beliefs. He is known as the mighty warrior angel who defeats Satan and eradicates lower negative energy from the world. Painters have depicted him as fierce, powerful, and courageous in the face of adversity.

We very often see him equipped with his sword of light and an army of fearless angels behind him. This is the essence of Michael, who is the leader of the 15 and all beings, who stands for truth, righteousness, light, and love.

I'm going to level here with you and say that simply put, Archangel Michael is an absolute badass. He represents the unyielding fight against the dark and his no tolerance for bullshit of any kind has him standing out from the rest of the heavens as the no nonsense, don't stop when you're tired, stop when you're done warrior. Things for him are black or white, and there is no such thing as a gray area. His job is to eradicate anything that is not of the light. He stands for ultimate truth, safety, protection, and relentlessness.

Archangel Michael teaches you how to be the leader of your own life by taking 100% responsibility for yourself. Everyone wants to be in charge of themselves until they find out how hard it is to be THAT accountable. Being accountable means that you no longer blame your life, hurts, brokenness, or issues on anything or anyone else. It means that you take massive action to heal yourself and forgive others so that you can step into your own power. And it means that you become self sufficient and self reliant- meaning that you are no longer going to give your power away to an outside source and will now acknowledge that everything you need is within you.

Leaders lead from the front, which means that they are willing to first do what they want their followers to then do. If you are the head of a business, household, store, group, organization, etc. you must be willing to show your team what must be done in order to ensure everyone's success. Think of King Arthur and the knights of his round table. In his search for the Holy Grail, Arthur doesn't just send out his army with a list of orders. He journeys with them, leading his knights by example and including their wisdom and knowledge in his experience. Zig Ziglar said, "You will get all you want in life if you help enough other people get what they want." To me, this is the round table mentality. The leader isn't leading for the purpose of having followers; he's leading to pave the way for everybody to find their strength and their own success.

Leaders fearlessly take risks. They see risks differently than people who bow down to their fears of failing. A person facing risk from a place of fear may ask, "what if I do this?" And a myriad of frightful scenarios follow in their imagination. When they see all of the fear based possibilities, they stop. They perceive that the safer road is to quit before they even attempt anything. However, a leader will look at a risk and ask, "what if I *don't* do this?" and they will clearly see the success they won't achieve if they don't at least try. So, if you are looking at being a leader of your own life, or for others, you must understand what Archangel Michael understands. It's not about what you might lose if you do it. It's about what you're going to lose if you don't.

Archangel Michael as a human being... oy vey! First of all, you may not realize this, but most humans on this planet wouldn't appreciate Michael as a human as they do an Archangel. His intensity, and straightforwardness would intimidate many people, and his blunt to the point honesty would surely offend egos worldwide. However, with his high integrity, mastery in leadership and communication skills he would be someone you'd vote for, at least if he had the patience to deal with politics...which I am certain he wouldn't. But Archangel Michael as a human would definitely make a lot of waves.

Historically, the world cries for leaders, but destroys anyone who attempts to make the kinds of changes that are best for us. Joan of Arc carried the energy of Archangel Michael when she showed the unwillingness to hide or renounce her ability to see and hear angels and be guided into war under their mighty influence. And look what happened to her. Jesus was put to trial and then crucified for similar reasons. So I've decided not to give Archangel Michael much of a human persona in this book. Rather, I would like to spend time exploring how we can all embody him, as this might be a better way to get to know him and understand him. And so that we can all begin to be the leaders in our own lives.

In his spare time, I'm sure he'd love doing all the 'manly' stuff- watching sports, fixing things, admiring cars, and pumping iron at the gym. He is as masculine as the Archangels get. However, he wouldn't be the kind of masculine we might have been taught by society. If you can remember how I described the moon as feminine energy in Archangel Haniel's section, I would describe Archangel Michael's masculine energy as the sun. Healthy masculine energy is consistent, giving, generous, and hardworking. After millennia, the sun never says to the earth, "you owe me." No, the sun is simply bright, bold, and dependable because that's just what the sun does. Masculinity, in its purest form is just like that. It is the ability to lead, to give, and to produce without strings attached. Of course, the ability to be consistently generous not usually understood, and therefore nor would Archangel Michael be.

How You Can Be Like Archangel Michael

In order to be a leader like Archangel Michael, you must be willing to develop skills to focus. Archangel Michael cannot be distracted from his goal. You must dedicate yourself to your purpose and go after it as if you are starving for it. The ability to stay focused on your goal has to be unwavering. Leaders don't look to their left, or to their right to see who is running the race against them. Looking at opponents will slow you down and trip you up. If you ever find yourself comparing yourself to others, be like Archangel Michael and remember; Leaders focus on leading, losers focus on winning.

Above all, you must be brave. Archangel Michael, as the protector cannot waste even a second on fear. He sees the scariest things in the universe and without hesitation slays them with his mighty sword. Is he capable of feeling afraid? This I'm not sure of, however I believe that if he did ever get scared he would feel the fear and march forward anyway. Fearless actions don't mean that you're not feeling fear. They just mean that you aren't letting fear stop you. You can be like him when it comes to your own worst fears.

The first step is to just look at what scares you. Anytime you go into denial of something, or run away from your problems, they only get bigger. Remember the scary shadows under your bed or in your closet at night when you were a child? You can see now as an adult how harmless they truly are, but your fears made them so much worse. But in the moments when you were scared, you weren't aware that the fear itself is what drew out the worst of your imagination. You believed what fear whispered in your mind. It wasn't until you mustered up enough courage to turn on the light that you discovered the truth of the situation. When you stop running and you face your shadows, you turn on that light. What you'll find is that once you find the courage to look at your fears, it's never as bad as you imagined. What once seemed so real disappears within the light of your attention and awareness. You see that the monster in your closet, the one that tormented you for years, is simply a shadow of something smaller, and that shadow no longer exists with your light shining upon it. So, you can be like Archangel Michael and be brave

102

by acknowledging what scares you, but marching towards it anyway. Chin up, shoulders back, wings out, and sword drawn!

"A leader is best when people barely know he exists, when his work is done, his aim fulfilled, they will say: we did it ourselves."-Lao Tzu

The Mind State

Remember Your Why: The fear of the unknown is probably the most debilitating feeling. I see fear as a big scary monster, guarding the doorway to a treasure you deserve. Remembering why you want to overcome that fear is more powerful than the monster will ever be. Anytime you feel fear, just know that something amazing is behind it. It's a lot easier to look fear in the eye and take brave action when you remember your Why. Why did you want to be in a relationship? Why did you want to lose weight? Why did you start your own business? Why do you want to make certain changes? Why do you want to get better? Your Why is very often the driving force that gets you past the fear monster and into the open doorway to your treasure. Fear-monsters keep you from accessing self esteem, confidence, your life purpose, and your success. Sometimes it's is a matter of loving yourself more than you fear the monster.

Vulnerability: Only the brave and open hearted dare to allow themselves to be vulnerable. It takes a lot of courage to remove your walls and expose your humanness. It also takes an incredible amount of discipline to keep your defense mechanisms in check. When I began to live a life of vulnerability, I had to really check to see who I was surrounding myself with. I made the decision that I no longer wanted to live with or around people who would make me want to put up walls or to shut down in any way. My circle of friends changed greatly when I made that decision. I removed harsh people from my life and made the decision to only surround myself with people who would honor my open and vulnerable heart. I renegotiated relationships with anyone who was judging me, disapproving of me, competing with me, or inviting drama of any kind into my life. This allowed me to take a deep breath and relax into relationships and be myself completely. Your true self is strong, honest, and open. The reward to being vulnerable is freedom, love, and a sense of inner "badass." It takes a lot of bravery to be vulnerable, but it's so worth it! You deserve to live life as your fullest, truest self, surrounded by people who will empower and accept you.

Co-operation: Everyone has something to contribute. By having a co-operative mind state, you will begin to look for how you can bring people together and explore ways you can all assist each other. Thinking that you have to do it all comes from the need to control the outcome and it may lead to power struggles, conflict, and competition. When you are focused only on your desired outcome and disregard others, you miss out on the many ways people around you can contribute. The idea here is to always look for win-win situations and outcomes that serve the whole. There is a positive resolution to all conflicts, and there is always a better way to do things- especially if you are willing to utilize everyone's gifts and talents.

The Work

Be a warrior, not a worrier! 80-90% of everything you worry about will never come to pass. Worry is the misuse of your imagination. Think about what you're afraid of and give yourself a reality check. If the worst were to actually happen, (and by the way, the worst your imagination can come up with is probably not a practical reality) would you be okay? Would you not be able to get back up, dust yourself off, and continue on? If the worst were to really happen, would you not find a new direction, experience, or friend to help you through? The fact is that you are far more resilient than your fearing mind will ever give you credit. Yes, the worst would suck, but you would get through it. We humans are like cockroaches. Look at everything we've been through on this crazy planet to evolve into what we are today. You can't get rid of us. Nothing can destroy you, and you are unstoppable.

Let us examine how we as humans deal with tragedies like terrorist attacks and natural disasters. While the worst is happening, we are quickly helping each other, finding escape routes, rebuilding, renewing, transforming, coming together, and overcoming. The very spirit of who you are is one of triumph. The purest essence of who you are comes out when everything goes wrong, and that is the essence of strength and bravery. Trust that these qualities are at your core and you have the real option to never stop because of fear. Remember who you are and your worries will be no more than an annoyance to be brushed aside. Know that under the worst pressure, you have within you what it takes to survive, persevere, and win.

Feel the fear and do it anyway! Write down three fears that are keeping you from moving forward. The first step to being brave is admitting what scares you the most. Doing this is like turning on that light to see what's really causing the shadows. You may be surprised at how liberating it feels to just write it down and look at it. You may even get some ideas about what your next steps are. Read over what you've written with the mind state that you are unstoppable. What you'll find is that your worries and fears mean nothing in the face of your bravery. There are possibilities for pain, but when you stand tall in your power and relentlessly fight for what you want, the possibilities for your triumph are even greater. If you want to take massive action in your life, don't stop when you're tired, worried, scared, frustrated or discouraged. Stop only when you are complete, and begin even when you are afraid.

Real Life

Years ago, I taught a "Connecting to the Archangels" workshop where we would go through each Archangel and discuss subjects similar to what is taught in this book. We were in the midst of a meditation that helped my students to connect to their angels when I felt a very powerful presence begin to guide my words. To this day, I will never forget the message that Archangel Michael so benevolently gave me to relay to my students.

"Be a lighthouse. Be a lighthouse with enough power to light up the entire night sky. Enough light to beam through thick murky fog and steer ships through rough and stormy seas. Your light, when given fearlessly and unconditionally is enough to light up the entire world. Lighthouses, as it is, are never built in easy, well-lit places. They are built in tough situations, dark rocky shores, and places where ships need light. Lighthouses never leave their position to go out into the storm to save ships... no that would be a catastrophe. No one would know where to go. Lighthouses simply just stand at their station, and they shine their light as far and wide as they possibly can. And you, as a lighthouse must do the same. You must make sure that your lens is clear of anything that would dim your light. Clear away the hate, clear away the judgments, clear away the self doubt and distractions. Don't go chasing people around giving unsolicited advice, telling them what to do, what books to read, what seminars to sit through. For, when you are in your joy, your bliss, your happiness and shining your light so bright, people will naturally be attracted to you. They will ask you what you are doing to be so happy and bright, and at that point you can tell them the story of a lighthouse that was built upon a dark rocky shore, and who recognized the need for light in that place. You can tell them the story of how this lighthouse cleared up its lens and fearlessly, with no apprehension beamed brightly for the lost ships. Your story is the most powerful thing you have, and it is what you get to share to those who are attracted to your light. After all, wasn't it someone else's story at some point that steered you in? Someone was a lighthouse for you. Now it's your turn. Be a lighthouse."

From that class on, I have always loved to relay the message of the lighthouse to my clients and students. Life is never easy for lighthouses who withstand storms and dark nights. But perhaps you-as the lighthouse- were built there because you could handle it. The best option isn't to become dark yourself, but to do whatever it takes be the brightest beacon out there.

Archangel Michael's Message To The Modern World: *"You have the power, all you need is silence. In silence you will quiet the voice of fear and refocus on what you really want and why you want it. Once you remember who you are, and you are clear about your intentions, nothing in the universe has the power to stop you. You cannot fail. All your seeming failure means is that it is time to redirect, refocus, and continue on. When you live your life this way- on purpose- you will find yourself in a position of leadership because you will naturally inspire those around you. Never let leadership get to your head. To lead is to serve, and to serve is the highest honor you will ever fulfill. Service to your friends, family, and acquaintances will challenge your ego, but it will develop you in ways nothing else can. It will require that you develop a no tolerance for BS from yourself or from anyone else. Remember that you are safe, you are protected, and at your weakest moment, don't quit. Get quiet.*

You are responsible for your life, and if you're sitting around waiting for someone to save you or to fix you, you are wasting your time. Only you have the power to make your life what you want it to be. God is not going to appear on your doorstep with money, fame, a lover, and a magic pill to make you gorgeous. But you do have ideas- so many ideas. And you do have support- so much support. This world offers more resources than you even need. You have no excuses- you have only fear to conquer. What are you waiting for? Get out there and just be brave!"

Questions To Consider: Are you clear about who you are? Do you want to find out what you're capable of, and what you truly desire? Are you willing to put yourself out there as the voice of reason and truth? Are you ready to look your fear monster in the eyes and claim what it guards? Are you ready to wield your own fiery sword of truth and light and be the brave leader you are meant to become? These are questions to ask yourself if you would like to stand tall and fearless like the valiant warrior, Archangel Michael.

Chapter 10

Archangel Raguel- The Law

Everything Happens For A Divine Reason And In Divine Timing

It seems as though the wind constantly blew there. A small lake in the middle of nowhere, surrounded by weathered trees with their rough looking leaves. It was a rather harsh part of the planet, some might even call it ugly. Except for one time of year, when the lily pads and lotus flowers bloomed and beautifully changed the entire landscape. It is at the very bottom in the deepest muddiest part of the lake our story takes place. A small little seed had fallen deep down into the slimy depths and was just beginning to sprout. As it poked up from the sludge, the little sprout noticed it was in a very dark, gloomy, watery place. "Oh my," It thought. "I am so very dark and gloomy." You see the seed did not see itself, and so it perceived that it was like everything it saw.

As the days and weeks went by, the sprout grew taller and taller. Growing up in the dark murky waters, it developed a sadness that made it want to sleep and dream of being beautiful. The little sprout would look up and dream that one day he would be tall enough to see what was above the muddy waters. There were fish in the lake who also felt the ugliness of their surroundings and assumed they were ugly too. This made them act ugly. The fish were mean and cruel to each other. They would bump into the sprout without a pardon.

When the sprout got even taller, he could see an old rotting tire that someone had thrown into the lake. The smell of old rubber and slime filled the water and for a couple of weeks, the sprout didn't think he could handle it. All he knew is that

109

he wanted to see what was above the surface. When the sprout got even taller, he began to sense and see other sprouts around him who were growing towards the surface. He tried to talk to them, but they too were overcome by shadows and darkness. It seemed as though the sprout had no friends at all.

One day, the sprout woke up to find that things looked different. He couldn't see the bottom of the lake anymore, although he was definitely still attached. He realized that he was sitting just beneath the surface of the water. The surface was crazy with light and movement. Little waves lapped on top of him, seemingly pulling him upwards and through the top and into the light. Within a few days, the sprout had broke free of the water and there was a feeling of expansion he had never experienced before. Almost as if he were coming apart, yet somehow staying together. There was also a new feeling of air, and the smell was floral and sweet. As he gazed around him, he could see lily pads and flowers everywhere. It was then he realized that he was not the murky deep water after all, but that he was just experiencing it. He wondered what exactly he was. As he looked down into the reflection of the water he saw the most beautiful, exquisite lotus flower. Is this me? He gasped! Just then, there was a wind that carried the giggles of the other flowers. They too, had broken free from the darkness and were reveling in what they too understood. The handsome lotus now stood as tall as he could, roots firmly deep beneath the lake, head basking in the sunshine and beauty all around him. "I am not the darkness, I am not the mean fish, I am not the rotting tire, I am not the scared sprouts. Those were just things happening around me. I am and have always been a magnificent lotus and it is I who make this place beautiful!"

Archangel Raguel is the angel of Divine Law, Order, and Sacred Contracts. Because our personal lives and the world around us change so drastically sometimes, it is easy to think that this universe is nothing but a series of chaotic events. The idea that things just randomly happen to you keeps you powerless and a victim to circumstance. However, if you are open to understanding that even though some things don't make sense, things happen in their divine order and timing. Like the lotus flower in the descriptive story, there is timing to our growth. There is always a reason we meet people in our lives and for the experiences we have. Our freedom lies within how we chose to act, react, think, and perceive the experiences in our lives.

Divine Contracts

You are limitless. You are so much more than a body that walks around and performs random actions until it dies. Not only are you more than your body, you are more than your name, your face, your status, your title, your accomplishments. You are more than any label your family or society has placed upon you. You are an infinite soul who has chosen to be born into a life that will give you the kinds of challenges that will help you to learn and grow. These situations that are set up before you are born are called Divine Contracts.

A Divine Contract is an agreement you made with another person or even an organization before you came to this life. You set up who would be your allies and who would be the bad guys so that you could play out the experiences and scenarios necessary to your growth. If you haven't read the book "The Little Soul and The Sun" by Neale Donald Walsch, I highly recommend that you do to learn more about Divine Contracts. It tells an endearing story of a little soul who was having a conversation with God about coming to earth to experience life. The little soul can't wait to develop things about himself so that he can be more like God. When God asks the little soul what aspect he was most excited about learning about, the little soul eagerly says he can't wait to learn the aspect of forgiveness. God then proceeds to tell the little soul that there was a problem because God only creates perfection, from love and light. Presently, there would be no one who could do anything "wrong" or "bad" to provoke the little soul to learn how to forgive. When the little soul is sad about this fact, another little soul steps forward and offers to help by being the one who will do something that the little soul can forgive. They are innocent, excited, nervous, and naive as the second little soul puts on a dark cloak and begins to hide herself so that the first little soul won't recognize her. As they both ready themselves for life, the second little soul asks one thing of the first, who innocently tells her, "anything!" She says that in order to do this "bad" thing, she will have to forget who she truly is, and that she is made in love and perfection. She asks that in the moment she does her worst to the first little soul, that he please try to remember who she really is because it will be her who will be lost. And the contract is made.

The book is a real tear jerker; I highly recommend that you read it with someone in mind who's hurt you. If you are intent on continuing to blame that person for your pain, you'll probably hate the message, but read it anyway. Understanding Divine Contracts gives you an "angel's eye view" to the dramas in your life. People show up and they play roles, some less attractive than others. You are playing a role too. Perhaps you've had to be the one in the dark cloak giving someone else an opportunity to embody forgiveness. My strong faith in Divine Timing & Order and in Divine Contracts has delivered me through horrific and terrifying events. By seeing the roles we are all playing while remembering my limitlessness, I have been able to heal, forgive, and choose to gain the lesson and wisdom within the hurtful times rather than wallow in pain.

On a more positive note, we also make happy Divine Contracts with many people. That is why you can meet someone and instantly know you are kindred spirits, ready to support each other as if you've known each other for ages. Everyone in our lives has a contract to be a certain player in our growth. So, instead of blaming, shaming, and judging, ask yourself what you need to learn, and what Diving aspect you wanted to embody through the relationship.

Divine Timing & Order

I once got into an argument with a family member over this next section. In a passing comment, I mentioned that "everything happens for a reason". This set them off as though I had just told them the sky was falling. They even went as far as to say, "You mean if I cut you with a knife, right now, it was *meant* to happen?" I'm laughing as I think back at how immature this conversation was, however I've run into many people who want to challenge these truths. My response is always the same: you can keep your opinions and give up your peace, and life will go on exactly as it always has. Or you can let go of your opinions and decide that you don't know everything, and life will unfold in ways beyond your wildest dreams.

Here are the four pillars of Divine Timing & Order:

1. When something is supposed to start, it will begin.
2. Everything that has happened in your life was supposed to occur just as it did or it wouldn't have happened.
3. Everyone in your life is supposed to be in your life or they wouldn't be there.
4. When something is supposed to end, it will end.

It serves our faith to trust these truths. Archangel Raguel is known as the angel who restores faith after tragedies by empowering us with these truths. He is seen holding the scales of justice. He reminds us that karma is very real, what goes around comes around. Therefore, it is best to focus on forgiving, and getting through whatever someone has done to you, and allowing the natural consequences and forces of the universe to deliver. Acts of revenge come from not having faith in the fact that the universe is a just and fair place, and therefore you have to take matters into your own hands. Revenge will never heal you. It will never make YOU better. Your faith and focus on your growth is the only way to redeem anything. Instead of becoming ugly in the midst of injustice, become beautiful. The best feeling is when someone who hurt you sees you doing better than you did before. Taking your power back is probably the best kind of karmic consequence possible! Watching your haters watch you conduct your life with grace, poise, and ease after they've done their worst is simply delicious. Balance your own scales by being triumphant!

If Archangel Raguel were human, he would be justice in action. Obviously involved in law, he would be someone we could count on and trust to make decisions that were in our best interest. He would challenge the majority of lawmakers and his honesty and loyalties would not be for sale. He would retain his power by continuing to state the truth, and not taking any backlash personally. I don't think he'd be an everyday lawyer because arguing or debating on small issues would not be his priority. As a man who holds his power and poise under pressure, I imagine he would be someone who was a part of creating and enforcing laws, policies, and bills on a higher level of justice.

Archangel Raguel would most likely live in downtown Washington DC where he could easily have access to everything going on inside and around our nation's capitol. He would have a keen sense of injustice and fervently fight for balance within our legal system. He would have a massive impact on the Supreme Court, perhaps acting as an advisor and urging our lawmakers to quit accepting bribes and gifts for their votes. His name means, "Friend of God", and so I believe his people skills would be remarkable. He would be likable, even if he were standing at the opposite side of your cause. All in all, he would make shocking revelations as he exposed dishonesty, injustices, and offences against our laws, while caring deeply for the structure, boundaries, and safety laws are intended for.

Archangel Raguel would be seen in nice suits, carrying a briefcase, and driving a very nice car. He would look professional and exude great power and knowledge. Yet, there would be a twinkle in his eye along with the seriousness on his face. You would immediately trust him. He would probably like golf and tennis and be a member of a club where he could socialize with other go-getters. Among his family and friends, he would be the first one to settle an argument and diplomatically restore peace, however much he enjoyed a good, healthy debate. At the end of the day, Archangel Raguel would feel the peace that comes from making a difference. He would feel that justice was real, and that he was a part of bringing balance and order to our society. He would probably stay up late looking over cases, bills, and legal papers with a notepad to write down his thoughts and he would love every minute of it!

How You Can Be Like Archangel Raguel

It is so easy to accept the Circle of Life when it is being sung in "The Lion King." It all makes sense- that is until you are face to face with Divine Order that seems to go against your own personal agenda. The most difficult thing humans deal with is the fact that we aren't in charge of everything. There is a time for all seasons, all beings, and even all beliefs. When you understand the 4 pillars of Divine Timing and Order, it is easier to accept things as they happen- even the hard things. As I have discussed in earlier sections of this book, when we accept things as they are, we can allow our authentic emotions to emerge and move forward. Healing just can't happen until acceptance is had. Very often, it isn't so much the event itself, but our resistance to the event that causes the most pain. Wishing something would or wouldn't happen in the face of a reality that says otherwise only puts more fire to an already burning anguish.

In order to bring justice and truth to light, Archangel Raguel would see things exactly as they are- not just as he would hope. In order to be like him, you are required to open your eyes fully and push all of your personal agendas and desires aside, at least long enough to see and accept the truth. Seeing the truth of any situation will liberate you and set you free no matter how much you want things to be different. Once you are fully aware of the truth and have accepted it, it is up to you to take action to rectify, balance, expose, and make things right based on what IS. There is no greater place of power than this from which to make great change happen.

"All the world's a stage, and all the men and women merely players: they have their exits and their entrances; and one man in his time plays many parts, his acts being seven ages."-William Shakespeare

The Mind State

Procrastination: I would like to discuss the subject of procrastination here because it seems to be primarily an issue with timing, and Archangel Raguel is the archangel of Divine Timing and Order. I would like you to consider what you have learned about Divine Timing and Order and ask yourself if, under the 4 pillars, procrastination could even be possible? If everything begins and ends when it is supposed to, then what is really going on when you are seemingly procrastinating? Let's explore the method behind your madness.

The biggest culprit of procrastination is fear. Maybe you don't feel like you are ready or maybe you don't feel you have the skills or knowledge to do what you want to do. In the frame of Divine Timing and Order, all things happen in steps. If you find yourself procrastinating, maybe it is because there are steps you are missing or not seeing. Perhaps you need to obtain more resources, people, support, or assistance from others in order to overcome your fears and take the next steps towards your goal.

If you pay attention, you will find that there is an ebb and flow to life. Sometimes it seems as if we have so many things going on, we barely have enough time to think. Other times, things slow down and we feel restless. This is where the phrase, "when it rains it pours" comes from. We all recognize that sometimes a lot happens, and other times not so much. I've come to learn that usually right before everything picks up, there is a lull- like the quiet ocean before the tide begins to roll back in.

There is always calm before the storm. There is a good chance that your case of procrastination is right on time. Trust life when it tells you to rest, trust life when it tells you to work. Pay attention to what life is telling you so that you don't go into the unnecessary guilt and shame that come from thinking you are procrastinating.

Choices: Making decisions can sometimes be so hard that we choose to remain in indecisiveness instead of making a choice and moving forward. Remember that by not making a decision, you are making the decision to stay stuck.

My favorite question to ask myself when faced with a decision is, "How will I feel about this situation a year from now?" Looking into the long term effects of a decision is a good idea, and even if you can't see the absolute outcome of your choices, you can usually make a guess at how you will feel about your choice in the long run. Worrying about making the wrong choice can often result in making your choice in the spirit of fear- which rarely turns out as a benefit.

The best way to make a choice is to get still, take some deep breaths, and ask yourself that question slowly. "How will I feel about this situation (or myself) a year from now?" Pay attention to how your body reacts to the question, you may have to reword it a few times to get to the core of what it is you are really deciding. Then answer yourself in different ways, again slowly. Pay attention to how each answer feels, and what kinds of fears come up with each answer. Be creative and imagine different kinds of scenarios, making up some silly, crazy, or outlandish outcomes in your mind. They don't all have to seem possible, easy, or attainable; this is simply an exercise of the imagination to tap into creativity. Let your mind drift into scenarios where money, time, and circumstance didn't have an impact on your decisions. Dream up outcomes that serve everyone involved and let your mind wander into possibilities. Of all of the answers you come up with, pay attention to how your body feels and which decision brings you the most peace. From your point of stillness and infinite possibilities, you will see what step to take next.

Purpose: Every situation and person is placed in your life with a purpose. It may be to strengthen you, offer you an opportunity to resolve the past, or for pleasure and enjoyment. The main purpose of your soul experience is to learn forgiveness. It is also to engage in what brings you joy, satisfaction, and fulfillment. When you seek out these qualities, you will be led towards situations and people who will give you the opportunity to fulfill your purpose. Ask yourself right now, "what situations and people have given me the opportunity to fulfill my purpose to forgive, experience joy, satisfaction, and fulfillment?" The answer to that question is another clue to what you came to this life to do.

Knowing that there is a greater purpose behind certain painful or negative situations can sometimes help us get through the hardships and into a place of clarity and understanding. If anything, let it comfort us to know that everything, even though we may not see it right away, is happening for a higher reason. We are being taught, cultivated, developed, and even though it may not seem like it at the time, we are becoming better and stronger through the challenges. Everything has a purpose. Knowing this is the faith that gets you through.

The Work

It is time to align yourself to Divine Timing. When you are in alignment with Divine Timing, you always seem to be at the right place at the right time. Synchronistic events happen around you and it seems as if everything you need just pops up into your life at the absolute right time. First, this requires that you honor everyone's time.

It's important to realize that time is valuable. It is the one thing that can never be given back to anyone, so please make the commitment to show up on time- perhaps even early- to all scheduled events and appointments, even if they are casual. Being punctual is impressive, and it makes you feel good. If you are constantly running late, you probably feel bad and are constantly apologizing for putting people out. This can be a sign that you are out of alignment with Divine Timing. If you are running late for anything, ask yourself why. Are you scared to be where you need to be? If you weren't able to use the excuses you do for being tardy, what would your real reasons be? For instance, if traffic, work, babysitter, boss, or previous engagements were not a factor in controlling your time, what would you say the real reasons behind your timing issues were? Dig deep. Are you sabotaging friendships or opportunities? Are you attempting to control situations or people? Perhaps you just have too much on your plate and are drowning in overwhelm? Timing issues are a big deal and can reveal a lot of discord in your life. Really looking at how punctual you are will help you prioritize and let go of any drama, chaos, and negativity that disrupts your ability to show up as your best self and on time.

Sometimes we step out of sync with Divine Timing when we haven't been out in nature in a while. Nature is connected to Divine Timing. Everything in nature ebbs and flows, grows and dies, and changes according to Divine Timing. If you feel off, and like you are out of step, go walk barefoot on grass, dirt, or sand. Stand next to a tree, or a river or anywhere you feel like you can connect back to nature. Visualize roots coming out of the bottom of your feet and planting yourself firmly into the soil and feel yourself become connected, calibrated, and aligned again. See yourself showing up on time to work and events. Feel how good it is to arrive early relaxed, and easygoing. Imagine yourself having plenty of time all day every day to do the things you have to do and want to do, and see yourself going to bed at a good hour, feeling accomplished. You may have to do this several times, but the more you do it, the more you will begin to see these images becoming your everyday reality!

Remember that you get a brand new 24 hours every new day! Spend your hours wisely, and it will be like an investment that gives you more time in the coming days! Spend your hours poorly, and you are robbing your bank and it will feel as though you never have enough hours.

Ponder the four pillars of Divine Timing and Order. How do they affect your perception of who is in your life, and events that have taken place? Write down any areas of your life that you can now accept and cease being victim to by honoring the four pillars. For instance, if something was supposed to happen and you've been playing the victim to it, identify what lesson, attribute, or virtue must you attain in order to accept it and move on? Like the little soul in the sun, perhaps it is forgiveness. Or maybe you are to acquire strength, perseverance, unconditional love, self love, faith, charity, dignity, nobility, or courage. This is real hardcore angel work! It requires that you trust the process of life so fervently, that you let go of your need to blame anyone or anything anymore. In doing so, you will become the outstanding benevolent being you truly are meant to become!

Real Life

When I got pregnant at 18 during my senior year of high school, the first response from everyone around me was that it was a horrible thing. Because of the timing of my pregnancy, it was judged and I was persecuted. There was a lot of judgment and concern surrounding the fact that I was still a child myself and whether I would be able to raise a baby on my own. I don't blame anyone for having their opinions about my situation. Teen pregnancy is a hard subject, and looking back I can admit that I had no idea what I was about to embark upon. However, what many people in my life failed to realize is that it was the absolute perfect timing for me and my baby.

There are no accidents in this very intelligent universe. The road I was on before I became pregnant was paved with chaos and disaster. I was using drugs, smoking, drinking, contemplating suicide, and crying out for help and for someone to love and accept me. Who better to unconditionally love and accept me than a baby? I had no idea how I was going to be a mother when I clearly lived an out of control life, but the news of my baby changed everything. I finally had found a reason to be "good." I had a reason to live.

The adults in my life tried with all their might to convince me to give my baby up for adoption. I was even taken to very high pressure adoption agencies that validated my fears of not being able to provide a good life for my child. They painted a perfect picture of doing the "saintly" and "unselfish" thing by giving my baby to better people. Every influence in my life pointed to a distrust in Divine Timing and Order. During countless nights of feeling confused, unsupported, alone, and like a horrible failure, I finally came to the conclusion that I wanted to keep my baby. I decided to beat the odds and learn all there was to know about being a mother. I quit smoking and partying, left several of my friends, dove deep into parenting books and listened constantly to baby experts. For the first time in my life, I began taking care of myself and I got very serious about creating a better life. I vowed to do whatever it took to prove all of my naysayers wrong.

Nineteen years later, my son is still the best thing that has ever happened to me. We grew up together. I was young enough to enjoy being on the floor playing with him and watching his children's shows. He will always be the first person in my life that I was open to receiving unconditional love and acceptance from, and he has been my compass and grounding rod. Once my family saw how much I had changed in order to be his mother, I received the support and respect I deserved. There is no doubt in my mind that I was the perfect mother for him. I lovingly tell him that all of the mistakes I made while trying to raise him only gave him the proper learning experience of life and made him stronger! The challenge of being a young single mother is a huge part of who I am today. I wouldn't be here writing this book were it not for the Divine intervention of my baby's arrival. I shudder to think where I might be had I given in to all of the pressure to give him up. Yes, we had some very hard times and I made so many mistakes. There were times I didn't know what we would eat or how we would survive. I had to grow up fast and learn how to do things the hard way. I knew nothing about managing money, doing laundry, or even how to change a diaper! But I was willing to learn. And at the end of the day, no matter how hard life got for us, at least we had each other. My son was no mistake; he came at the absolute perfect time for US.

Archangel Raguel's Message To The Modern World: *"Faith in Divine Order and Timing takes a tremendous amount of strength. Sometimes you are left wondering why painful experiences happen. Yet, you are often disappointed when an explanation of why something happened does not give you peace. This is because knowing the reasons why we experience hurt won't change what happened. Letting go of the pain, being willing to forgive and heal, and choosing peace over the need for an explanation ultimately provides the relief you seek. Remember that life may give you a tough hand, but you are tougher. With every obstacle you encounter, know that you have what it takes to overcome it!"*

Questions To Consider: What have you been judging as bad timing? Do you trust the order of things? Who are the people in your life who showed up as the "bad guys" and what virtues are you willing to acquire in order to better yourself? What roles are you playing in another person's life? Are you involved in a legal battle? If so, what does justice and fairness really mean to you? Are there laws that you feel passionate about supporting? These are some questions to ask yourself if you want to be like the fair and just Archangel Raguel.

Chapter 11

Archangel Raphael- The Healer

Heal Thyself

She carefully turns the warm mug in her hands and brings it up to her face to inhale the sweet, healing scents. A flood of the smell of fresh herbs and delicate blossoms dance and swirl through her body. Eyes closed, she imagines what the sky would look like above the clouds; starry, magical, eternal. She lets the steam fill the empty space in her chest and in this moment, she is whole. It is a moment where illness does not exist, pain is far away. Her body is relaxing, joints let go, and neck opens. Breathing in her freedom, she is finally safe to let her wings unfurl. Carefully they unbind themselves from her shoulder blades and slowly unravel like blooming rose buds. The release from being bound makes her pink lips joyfully turn upwards. From behind her rise two glorious, pure white, downy feather wings. Lifting her chin, her wings stretch upwards and awaken from their long slumber. Eager to fly, she sets her mug down at her feet just as they lift from the ground. Her healing has come, she is now free. Free to be who she is, go where she must go, and do the things she was born to do.

Archangel Raphael is "Heaven's Healer." His name means "God Heals." He is known as "heaven's physician" who comes to the aid of those who suffer from physical, mental, and emotional illness. He also helps us to overcome addictions and unhealthy cravings. There are many stories about Raphael where people have recounted seeing him in their times of physical sickness and suffering: doctors who admit they feel a heavenly presence guide their hands during surgeries, EMT's who witness miracle healings at the hands of some angelic encounter. His presence, whether you believe in angels or not, has been responsible for humanity's faith in healing. Many doctors and healers will attest that faith is truly what heals.

Archangel Raphael is also known for healing animals and pets. He reminds us of how important and amazing our animal friends are. Animals are like angels; they are here to help open and heal our hearts. They teach us unconditional love, patience, and kindness. Forming a relationship to any animal is so special and wonderful. You can also learn a lot about yourself from your pets. As you'll read later in my "Real Life" story of this section, my dog showed signs of sickness and depression when I was going through a health challenge. There are many animals whose life purpose involves the helping and healing of humans. These would include seeing-eye dogs, cats who purr on the laps of the elderly in retirement homes that help to lower blood pressure and stress, and horses who help survivors of abuse to trust again. There are many agencies that train and promote healing through animals and if this is something you feel interested in, definitely look into it. The rewards for working with, for, and on behalf of animals are priceless!

Healing is a controversial subject. In today's modern world, we have so many medical and non medical options and so many different experiences that the process of healing has become confusing and complicated. The actual act of recovery is surrounded in controversy and skepticism. Between religious, political, and social commentaries on the subject, the conversations surrounding how one goes about healing their body can get so heated it can destroy relationships. Do you take the prescriptions or do you improve your diet? Do you sit in a sweat lodge or do you read the bible? Do you get Chemo or do you get massage and Reiki? Do you take herbs and teas or do you pop the pills? Do you improve your quality of life or do you spend it in the hospital? Which hospital offers the best quality of life? Do you depend on Doctors or do you seek healers? Green tea or the flu shot? Take a trip to the health food store, or pharmacy? And above all, who is going to preach to you, tell you what you should do, diagnose you, or shame you when you don't do it their way? Actually, who is going to support you? Whew! Getting sick and finding a cure is tiring! As if getting a diagnosis isn't enough, now you have to deal with ALL of the controversy and confusion about your next steps.

This is why I'm not going to go into healing and medicine in this book. I am someone who started in the medical field as a nurse, lab and X-ray tech; then decided to get a masters certificate in Bio-Energetics, which is the study of life, herbs, and homeopathy; then decided to become a hands on healer and Reiki master and teach about energy and angels. I've been all over the board. I have seen too much on all sides to argue one way or the other. I will however say this, and I wish everyone would honor this code: Manifesting a disease or illness AND healing it is PERSONAL. The "right" way is the way the sick person decides is best for them and that is the end of the story. I've seen miracles and seeming disasters on all sides, and I am convinced that within both the miracle and the disaster lies what the individual requires in order to learn, grow, live or die. If you see someone making choices with their life and health that differ from the ones you might make, you have two choices: You can choose to support them in their personal journey, or you can lovingly detach from their decision. Your choice is also completely personal, and it is your right as much as theirs to make. It is not our place however, to tell anyone that their choice is wrong. If nothing else, we can take every person's healing journey as learning experiences and opportunities to reassess our own beliefs and be open to change.

If Archangel Raphael were human, he would find himself a professional in the medical field and be extremely passionate about preventative medicine, which is taking care of the body so that it doesn't experience illness. He would also be interested and concerned with healing the relationships between us and our bodies. He would be a bestselling author on the subject, and perhaps even have his own medical talk show so that he could reach the masses with helpful healing advice. He could also have his own health program that would include nutritious meals and a workout plan to maximize awareness, options, and optimum health. He would definitely include animal health to his list of credentials, as he would be just as caring towards our animal friends as he would be to us.

Archangel Raphael would be the perfect picture of health. Radiant skin, a bright smile, healthy eyes, and a strong, toned, healthy body. He would be extremely careful about what he put into his body because he would understand that food is like fuel. If you put bad fuel in a car, it doesn't operate right, and the same goes for your food. He would love to cook healthy meals, and be involved in many different things from sports to outdoor activities in order to keep his body exercised.

Archangel Raphael is also the healer of relationships, so he would be in a loving soul mate relationship with a big happy and healthy family around him. That's right; Archangel Raphael would definitely be a big hearted, committed, and dedicated family man! He would provide for his family a nice house and they would take fun vacations around the world where he could travel and speak about health and wellness. Everywhere he went, he would make a difference in someone's life by either helping them to heal their heart, or take their physical health to the next level.

How You Can Be Like Archangel Raphael

Have you been thinking about making a diet or lifestyle change? If you want to be like the healthy, happy, and fit Archangel Raphael, you owe it to yourself to follow through on those inner promptings. Taking care of your health would be first priority if you want to be like Raphael. Making changes is easy when you love and accept yourself. You will find the time, energy, and knowledge to make those changes when they are your top priority.

Many people who study health related subjects such as exercise and fitness, nutrition, meditation, and natural medicine feel a calling to not only apply it in their own lives, but to help others make healthy changes as well. If you are someone who would like to help others heal themselves or become healthier, then it's time to begin! Just like the rest of the Archangels, Raphael wouldn't wait around for circumstances to be "perfect" to get started on his desires. He would passionately jump in! What kind of health related interests do you feel drawn to? What kinds of books, people, mentors, education, certifications, etc are required for you to attain in order to do what you would like to do? There's no time to waste once you get clear about what you want to do and how you want to do it. If you want to be like Raphael, get started now!

If you are already a health practitioner of some sort, remember that there is always something more to learn, apply, and teach. The health and wellness field is constantly evolving as both science and medicine continue to make advances and new discoveries. You can never know everything there is to know, and Archangel Raphael as a healer would be on the leading edge of new information and current ways of practicing his art. So please never stop learning. Your clients and students will thank you for all of your efforts to stay ahead of the game and be knowledgeable of the best ways to approach their health.

As mentioned, Archangel Raphael is a lover of animals as well as health and healing. Our animal friends deserve as much love, healing, and support as we do. If Archangel Raphael were human, he would be a huge advocate against animal abuse, poaching, and the mistreatment of animals. One of the best things you can do is remove your money and support from organizations that mistreat animals. The next step is to take action, sign petitions, and spread the word. I am convinced that every single human being has a calling to protect the animals and wildlife of this planet, and with that in mind, it may be easier than you think to take a stand and make a difference. Listen to your inner calling to care for the beings in our world. Pay attention to what sort of offences against animals really set you off. This is a clue to where you can begin to make a difference, as Raphael would if he were human.

"Listen to me…Your body is not a temple. Temples can be destroyed and desecrated. Your body is a forest- thick canopies of maple trees and sweetly scented wildflowers sprouting in the underwood. You WILL grow back, over and over, no matter how badly you are devastated." –Beau Taplin

The Mind State

Self Kindness: Your body has an intelligence of its own. It's breathing right now without your attention to your lungs. It is balancing blood sugar, healing scrapes and bruises, thinking, carrying information from cell to cell all on its own. Your body is an absolutely amazing thing that the medical and science fields have yet to fully understand! Your body is sending you information right now on what it needs in order to not just survive, but to thrive. Are you listening? When you don't listen to your body's messages, it has no choice but to get loud and angry. Just like any other relationship you are in, if you tried to speak to someone and they ignored you, how would you feel? What would you do if your life depended on their hearing you? The body will begin to send you physical messages through pain, illness, fat, and disease when it becomes desperate enough to grab your attention in hopes that you will finally make the necessary changes it needs you to make.

How do you talk to your body? How do you talk *about* your body? How would you feel if someone were to say the things about you that you say to and about your body? After all your body does for you to survive on this earth, don't you think it deserves some more credit? It is time to heal the relationship between you and your body. Look at it as a loving mammal who wants your love, acceptance, and attention. It has waited a very long time for you to consider it, care for it, and hear it. Your body wants nothing but to be able to communicate with you. Just like you would give your pet the food it enjoys and take it out for walks, decide that you will treat your body with similar consideration.

Our bodies crave sunlight, fresh air, foliage, and the minerals from dirt and sand. If you were to put a plant in a dark closet, it would die without having access to sunlight. Your body is the same way. When we find ourselves going from one building to the next, one car to the next, shielded with sunglasses, clothing, and sunscreen, we separate ourselves from our environment and this causes fatigue, sadness, and the feeling of darkness. Allow yourself to walk barefoot on the earth. Take time outside near trees, natural water, and in the sunlight and moonlight. Even people who live in cities can benefit from nearby parks. Consider bringing nature indoors by adding plants, fountains, crystals, beeswax candles, or flowers. You will definitely see an increase of energy and motivation when you honor your body's desire to interact with nature.

Addiction: When you hear the word addiction, you may immediately think of drugs, alcohol, sugar, or smoking. However, anything can become addiction. Physically, an addiction takes place when certain brain chemicals are replaced by a substance so that when the substance leaves the body, the person feels the withdrawal of those chemicals. Withdrawals can range from mild to severe in the person suffering the lack of chemicals from the brain and depending on the substance, it can take a few days to a few years for the brain to learn how to excrete the proper chemical levels again. With this definition, it is easy to understand that even emotions can be addicting, as every emotion creates a chemical reaction in the body to take place. This is why people can be addicted to things like drama, and knowingly or unknowingly be constantly causing drama in their lives in order to feed their addiction. Doreen Virtue wrote an amazing book that reveals the reasons why people get addicted to drama, and how they can recover. It's called "Don't Let Anything Dull Your Sparkle." She states that behind every highly dramatic person, there's an unresolved trauma. Drama is his or her way of asking for love, and begging for help and understanding. Doreen also wrote a powerful book called "Constant Cravings," where she addresses the chemical addiction people have to food and beverages.

The emotional issues behind addiction usually stem from unresolved issues, and a fear or unwillingness to connect to a higher source. That may seem like a bold statement, but think about it for a moment. If you are an addict, your initial pull towards the substance (whether it be food, drug, or drama) was because you needed either a distraction or to escape from an unresolved issue or fear. When you face your fears, heal the unresolved issues, and realize that everything you want from the substance can be given to you by a higher source, this begins the ultimate process of healing an addiction.

One of the main issues I've seen with addiction specifically when it is with a substance is loss in the ability to handle stress. I've come to understand that the ability to deal with stress is actually a gift from God and we exercise this gift every time we decide to address our stressful challenges without the aid of substances. Because the addiction actually numbs you from feeling anything, it is easier to pretend that problems and pain are not present. By ignoring the issues, you lose the lessons that are learned by sober people who face and heal their problems, past, and pain head on. I firmly believe that we are never given anything in our lives that we cannot handle. With every new challenge we face we literally develop the ability to overcome every single problem in our lives! However, instead of searching and developing that gift, so many run away and hide in some sort of numbing distraction that then becomes an addiction. Every addict has to realize that the problem and the pain are still present despite their attempts to divert the hurt. Those things will remain until we use God's gifts to overcome them. We all have to find healthy ways to deal with pain, stress, and strife. Right now, take a deep breath, and ask God and the angels to help you find healthy and productive ways to deal with your issues. By facing and healing our issues instead of choosing to run away and numb out, we build incredible strength, resilience, and become very powerful, mighty beings. If you really want to be a true badass like the 15, get busy healing your addictions and face the issues that you've been running away from.

The Work

Right now lower the book for a moment, close your eyes, and just take a deep breath. Your body LOVES to breathe deeply. Deep breathing relaxes you, slows down the racing heart, and lowers your stress hormones. Smile as you breathe deeply and this will tell your body that you are safe and happy. In return your body will excrete happy hormones and begin to repair and rejuvenate itself. As you breathe deeply, think about the following body wisdom from my dear friend, Radiance Larrabee, and feel appreciation for all your body does, is, has been, and will be.

"Your body has over 70 trillion cells.
There are thousands of complicated operations working in our bodies every moment of our lives.
Each cell has 10,000 more molecules than the Milky Way has stars.
That is definitely worth repeating:
Each cell has 10,000 more molecules than the Milky Way has stars, all working in harmony with each other.
Your heart beats 100,000 times every 24 hours.
Your heart pumps over 6,000 gallons of blood through your body each day.
Your spleen creates 3 million new red blood cells every second in order to replenish this blood.
Your cells and your body systems are in constant communication with each other.
Your body knows.
Your body knows.
Your body is intelligent, beyond our comprehension."- Jamie Radiance Marie Larrabee, Body Wisdom Coach.

Meditation: It seems as though the subject of meditation receives nothing but positive and raving reviews across the board from the medical and science field, to religious experts, to yoga studios. It might just be the one thing we can all agree on: that meditation has countless benefits. No matter what you use meditation for, you will see consistent results. In order to do the work in this section, I ask you to do a little bit of research for yourself to see what kinds of meditations would best benefit you in your life right now. Meditation simply means to be in the present moment with some sort of intent, whether it be to simply feel peace and oneness with God or to be present and visualize something you are manifesting. There are countless ways in which to use this powerful and amazing tool. Look into videos on the internet and classes in your community that teach you how to still and quiet your mind so that you can meditate on what it is you are wanting to achieve. Meditation, like anything new you try, will require practice and dedication, but don't worry that it will add more "things you have to do" to your plate. Instead, see meditation as a necessary way to upkeep your mind, body, and life. The little effort it takes to close your eyes, breathe, and be still will offer you much more in return. It will give you more than what you give to it- meaning that whatever time and effort you put into meditating, you will receive back in some way. If this doesn't make sense now, try it and you'll see.

Consistency: Consistency, with anything in your life is key to achieving desired results. Your health is no exception. When I was the owner of a health clinic, I saw many clients for nutritional counseling and natural medicine. I will boldly state that the clients who had the greatest healing, and who achieved their health goals, were the ones who stuck to their health programs. This is because you cannot do anything half-ass and expect to get more than half-ass results. As a health practitioner, I also learned that your body doesn't lie. When my clients would come in for their check-ups and complain that they weren't getting the results they wanted, it only took a bit of observation before I would see that they were being very inconsistent with their regimen. As much as I wish this were different, you can't eat well for only 3 days of the week and excuse the other 4, and still think you will notice a big difference in how you feel. What you'll probably experience is that you only felt great 3 days out of the week, instead of 7.

When it comes to your health and energy, you get what you give yourself. If you give yourself second-rate food, you will get second-rate energy. However, there are reasons you may feel inconsistent with your health. I've never met anyone that was sabotaging their health goals who didn't have some sort of underlying belief that they simply didn't deserve to be a healthier weight or feel better. If you have been inconsistent, look past the excuses you are telling yourself such as, "I don't have the time, money, support, or knowledge." Those excuses are the cover-up to what's really going on. The truth is, even if you had the time, money, support, knowledge and everything handed to you on a silver platter, you'd still come up with a reason why you couldn't be consistent because something else is going on deep inside of you. So do the work- be brave like the Archangels. Ask yourself what the real reasons are for you to quit, bounce from one plan to the other, and be inconsistent with your health. Be real with yourself. We all have our own fears of unworthiness, insecurities, fears, deep seated pain, and some people even have a history of abuse that tells them they don't deserve to live life and have great health. Your willingness to go deep and see the truth behind your inconsistency is what will set you free. Imagine finally addressing and getting help for these set-backs and finally living the healthy and happy life you deserve- the one that your angels and your Creator want for you!

The truth is that everyone has the potential to have vibrant health, no matter what your history is or what seems to stand in your way. It really is your Creator's desire that you be your own perfect health, weight, and vibrancy. When you see a happy healthy person, know that they are showing you what is possible. I've seen people who have severe handicaps, debilitations, and illnesses who still strive to meet their highest potential of health. In doing so, they inspire the people around them, and give themselves the quality of life that they deserve. Raphael would never let anything stand in his way, and he would push the people around him to do the same. Isn't it time for you to take a stand for your perfect health?

Animals and Nature: Heal your relationship to animals and nature. Your body needs companionship from animals and nature. Even if you have had a hard experience with an animal, it's time to heal your fears and accept the unconditional love and acceptance that our pets offer us. This doesn't necessarily mean you have to go out and get a pet. Being a pet owner is a huge responsibility and like any other relationship, it requires your time, attention, and effort. However, the rewards from allowing a pet to influence your life are remarkable. Studies show that positive interactions with animals can lower blood pressure, calm nerves, and instill joy. If you find that you can't own an animal, visit friends who do. Offering assistance at shelters, or just sitting at a park and petting the friendly dogs that approach you is a wonderful way to connect to animals. You can try horseback riding or feeding animals at a farm. Visit an aviary or butterfly atrium where you can interact with birds and beautiful insects. Anytime you have a chance to connect with an animal, do it reverently, openly, and joyfully and you will experience a relationship that benefits you perhaps more than any other.

Real Life

In the winter of 2012, I had a suspicious spot on my hip removed and found out it was cancerous and that there was lymph fluid around the site. It turned out to be cutaneous T-cell lymphoma (CTCL), a general term for T-cell lymphomas that involves the skin. Learning that this type of cancer could evolve into a more deadly form of Lymphoma, I was terrified. I was a single mother of two boys, living in my mother's home with no money, no insurance, and no support. I knew only one thing: I was not going to let myself die. This meant that I had to do a lot of soul searching and a lot of research. I decided not to tell anyone. It was right before Christmas and I wanted to give myself and my kids a beautiful holiday. I also told myself that I would do what felt right to me for 8 weeks and see where it got me before exploring some of the medication that is typically used for CTCL. I was open to pharmaceuticals, but I really wanted to try alternatives first. I truly believed that my body needed nurturing, kindness, and understanding, not chemicals, harsh treatments, and a cold sterile environment.

I share my healing journey not as a "this is how everybody should do it" method. Like I said, and will continue to point out, illness and healing are personal. I did what I had to do to heal- someone else will have to do what they have to do. The first thing I had to do was find out why I had manifested this disease. At the time, I was the healthiest person I knew! I was a vegetarian and ate very clean, I frequently worked out, took health supplements and vitamins, got plenty of sun, rest, sleep, and for the most part, I was pretty much living an organic, health conscious lifestyle. Because of this, I went through what I now call "Body Betrayal." Body Betrayal is when your body manifests something scary and you are shocked and offended. It's like, "Hey! WTF! Why are you doing this to me?"

What I had to come to terms with was that earlier that year, I had gone through a very painful divorce and had hit a very dark and dreadful place of lack, anger, hurt, and despair. I was depressed, and during this low I had rebounded into a very abusive relationship with someone whom I eventually ended up having to get a stalking injunction and protection order against. I felt trapped, and there were times I entertained the thought that dying would be a better alternative to the nightmare I was living. But I could never go through with it as long as my children needed me. And there was my dog, who I mentioned earlier. While I was able to put on a happy face for my kids and pretend that I was okay, she knew better. There was no hiding from my dog, and she also began showing signs of distress during this dark time. When I was completely honest with myself, I realized that my body was only doing what I had considered doing myself. This was not the first time I had suffered with suicidal thoughts in my lifetime. I remembered back to my cries for help as a teenager and realized that perhaps all of this "wanting out" finally manifested as an actual way out. I had to make a decision. As I looked into the faces of my boys, as I sat with my sweetheart dog, as I stared at my reflection in the mirror and remembered my life's purpose, it was clear to see that I had a life here worth living. If my body was just doing what I had been telling it to do, I knew that the first place I needed to start healing was my thoughts and my heart- pronto!

I found that laughter truly is the best medicine. I figured that if I had become sick because I was depressed and suicidal, than the remedy was to become happy. I added to my regimen television comedies (my favorites were The Big Bang Theory, Friends, and How I Met Your Mother), listening to empowering and motivating speeches on YouTube (Ted Talks are great), and watching comedians (Love Brian Regan). I spent time playing with sidewalk chalk, playing video games, coloring in coloring books, and taking fun bubble baths with my mermaid Barbie- a few things I loved to do as a child. I also included fun, lighthearted fun dancing like Zumba and Just Dance on the Wii. All of the laughing, dancing, and playing uplifted my spirits and made me feel free.

Besides happiness as my medicine, I also changed my diet, took herbs and supplements that specifically targeted cancer, detoxed, sweat, drank high ph water, took sea salt baths, and began to take care of myself like never before. I did yoga, spent time meditating and gently stretching my body. I also decided to do a series of far infrared therapy that consisted of lying in what's called a "hot house" for hours at a time. Far infrared technology is really amazing and something I suggest everyone look into. What I found in the 8 weeks of all of this was that my healing was not just for my body, but for my broken heart and spirit. I addressed many emotional issues, cried about things I had been avoiding, and forgave the people I had held grudges against. I noticed that as I began to lighten my heavy load of sadness and sickness, my dog also began to transform. The more alive I began to feel, the more she began acting like her playful doggie self again. My boys got me out of bed in the mornings, and my dog got me out of the house. Unbeknown to them, my little family became my greatest healers... they will never know. All in all, I chose to focus on my wellness, not my illness.

One day as I was meditating to soft music and repeating the mantra, "I choose life" a very kind thought entered my mind. It was simply, "I'll know I've healed when I can't stop laughing." It was a peculiar thought, but I rested with it anyway.

Eight weeks later I went in to have the Doctor remove more tissue around the site because he had not gotten all of it in the first surgery. He wanted to make sure there wasn't lymph fluid present anymore. I knew that if there was, I would be in for major blood work and medical treatments. But somehow I knew everything would be okay. When the report came back that I was clear, I felt every cell in my body celebrate. It was a real "cell-ebration!" I chose life, and I continue to choose life every day!

Since then, I have kept up my "happiness regimen." I have found that this world is not innately positive or uplifting, and that I have to make the time and effort to find motivation and laughter. Weeks after I was deemed clear, I heard a story I'd like to share with you. It's actually a twisted little story, (proving that my sense of humor is possibly more sick than my health now) and I doubt it's even true. It may not even be that funny, but for some reason it hit a funny bone with me and I got giggling so hard over it! That is when I knew I had truly healed... I just couldn't stop laughing!

The story goes that a man walked into his garden one day to find his dog with a piece of dirty fur in its mouth. Examination proved that the dirty piece of fur was actually a prize rabbit belonging to a little old lady that lived next door. It was very dead, although no obvious injury could be seen.

The man was horrified and felt terrible. He took the rabbit inside, shampooed and blow dried it, and then quickly snuck next door to put it back in the hutch before the neighbor got home.

A few hours later, he heard shrieking and screaming as the poor old woman saw her bunny dead in his cage. The man ran out to offer his guilty conscious the chance to comfort his neighbor.

"Oh, no," said the man. "How awful!"

"I don't understand!" Says the neighbor. "My bunny died yesterday morning and I buried it and now here he is back in his cage!"

As I've mentioned several times throughout this chapter, healing an illness is a personal journey. I cannot stress the importance of looking at disease as a dis-ease and to see it symbolically as well as literally. What I mean is that taking medicine is one thing, but getting to the core reason why an illness has developed will lead you to an overall healing that might not only increase the years of your life, but give you the quality of life you truly deserve. Your healing may be what sets you upon your path towards your life's purpose, and could potentially help many others heal their lives as well.

Archangel Raphael's Message To The Modern World: *"Your body is the greatest tool you have. It is capable of telling you when imminent danger is present, and it can adjust itself to almost any circumstance. Your life is not separate from your body. How you treat your body affects your entire life. By healing your body, you are maintaining the structure of your life. When your body is unable to carry out tasks, your quality of life diminishes. This is not our wish for you, and not the intention that your Creator had when your body was given to you. It is your responsibility to keep it healthy, and your privilege to have all of the experiences your body gives you. Think about how limited you are without transportation, and yet most people spend more time and attention on their cars than on their bodies. Just as if you must put good fuel in your vehicle and treat it with care, you must do the same, if not more for your body if you want to live the life you were born to live. Think of maintaining your body through nutrition, exercise, rest, and play like you would maintain a brand new vehicle of your dreams. Think about how proud you could be of your body, riding around in style, going where you want to go and doing what you want to do effortlessly and without care of pending illness. The better your health, the better your life!"*

Questions To Consider: Are you happy with the relationship you have with your body? Do you trust it? Have you been thinking of changing your diet, exercise, rest, and play? What is stopping you from attaining the health that you deserve for the life you were born to live? How much time do you spend in nature? Do you spend time with animals? Do you feel compelled to adopt a pet in need of a home? How can you support the wildlife and nature kingdoms of your world? What is the one thing you need to stop eating or engaging in TODAY? These are things to ask yourself if you want to be like the medicinal, healing, wise, and caring archangel Raphael.

Chapter 12

Archangel Raziel- The Professor

Some Things Are Not Meant To Be Understood, But Accepted

The young apprentice carefully stepped into the room and looked around. It was a whirlwind of everything magical. Dusty books were stacked up in piles and along large bookcases. The tables layered with parchment, odd shaped glass bottles, dried herbs, nuts, berries, twigs, and feathers. There was a dying fire in the hearth warming a large pot of something that smelled earthy and dense. The apprentice took out his pocket watch with a clammy hand and checked the time. Yes, it was the hour of which they said they should meet. His nerves were getting the best of him, surely the wise and powerful wizard would sense this weakness and be done with him at once. At that thought, the apprentice stood a bit taller and rolled his shoulders back. He took in the sweet scent wafting through the air for comfort. Suddenly, his eyes fell onto the most powerful item in the room, and he cocked his head slightly at the sight of it. The staff. Never had he seen it alone, for the wizard was never without it. It looked odd and a bit lonely leaning up against an old wooden bookshelf. Even without the wizard, anyone could tell this was no ordinary tree part. There was something about it that whispered "power." The room suddenly felt small and the apprentice realized his own discomfort being alone with this bold relic. His thoughts were interrupted by the incoming of a large black raven that noisily landed on the window making the apprentice jump and gasp in spite of himself. "Great," he thought gathering his wits, "Who am I kidding, I'm not cut out for this stuff. I can hardly stand alone in this room let alone learn how to be a great and mighty wizard." He took one last look around the room feeling torn, and with a sigh turned towards the door. To his astonishment, the wizard had filled the doorway with his presence without a sound. Blood rushed to the apprentices face as his mind ran with questions of "how long?", and "now what?"

"Humility." The word was enunciated and rolled out of the wizard's mouth like soft thunder. The whole room seemed to air out and become still. The wizard took a step forward and summoned his staff, which rose gently and glided into his outstretched hand. Clearing his throat, he spoke again. "You do not know which way to go- do you stay or do you yearn to know? You were born to be this, you know this to be true, you're scared of the unknown, and you don't know what to do. You were on your way, however I intercepted. Your first lesson is that some things are to just be accepted."

Archangel Raziel would best be described as the angelic version of Gandalf, Merlin, and the great wizards of lore and literature. He helps us to reevaluate our belief systems and increase our spiritual understanding. His name means "Secret of God" and he is most known for keeping the secrets of the Universe and honoring the Mystery of life. Archangel Raziel reminds us that our beliefs are relative to our understanding. In other words, the more you understand something, the more your belief will change about it. He holds the wisdom that things change when you change your mind about them and that it is important to understand that your beliefs are not concrete. In this way, you can remain open, teachable, and humble. To think you know it all is to cut yourself off from ever learning a better way. And there is always a better way.

Archangel Raziel helps us to accept the part of life that cannot be explained. It is in our nature to need to know how every little thing in the universe works. We have an insatiable need to know why things happen in our lives, and sometimes if we find ourselves feeling stuck and unable to make decisions because we can't explain something or figure something out. But there is magic in the mystery, and knowing everything takes away the magic that happens within the unknown. We don't have to know how miracles are performed, all we have to know is that miracles happen, and then we will see them everywhere we go. However, if we reject the mystery because we can't explain it, we will not recognize a miracle if it flashes right before our eyes. Believing is seeing- not the other way around.

Let's talk about your belief system for a moment. If "belief system" had an acronym it would, ironically, be BS. And that is essentially what it is. A belief is simply a thought that has been thought for so long that you have an emotional tie to it. If I think I'm ugly every day, and have an emotional tie to that thought, it will become a belief. Does that mean that my belief is correct? No. It's BS. Someone else might think I'm pretty and that is their BS. Your beliefs systems show up in everything you do, whether you want them to or not. It is like the food you eat. You can binge on unhealthy food privately, but the food you choose to eat will show up on your body. Just like your private belief systems will show up in your life. You can see someone's BS if you watch how they live life, especially when they are under stress. The same can be said by observing yourself. You may not even know what your inner beliefs are until you are challenged.

If you want to know what your true beliefs are, pay attention to the results you get out of life. If you are tired of negative patterns, you have to look honestly and directly into what you're actually getting out of life and start asking yourself what kinds of beliefs you might have that are setting you up for those results. If you are constantly broke or being used by people, you may have some deep beliefs that you deserve bad things to happen to you. I know it sounds crazy because to the logical mind it doesn't make sense to believe those things about you. However, these beliefs are often subconscious, and they influence you all the same. It might be time to consciously change the way you are subconsciously seeing and believing things about yourself in order to transcend your current BS.

If Archangel Raziel were human he would be one of those crazy, overly passionate university professors who would seem to be all over the place with enthusiasm and extremely deep thoughts. You would want to sit in his class and listen to his lectures all day because even through his extravagance, his teaching style would encourage your learning and understanding, and you too would become passionate about any subject he taught.

Archangel Raziel would be a fan of art, history and science, but fascinated with ancient history, and scientific theory. He would definitely travel the earth to witness strange and unexplainable sights left by aliens and the ancient cultures we have yet to understand. Whereas some professors and scientists shy away from the unexplainable, Archangel Raziel would LOVE the mysteries of the universe! He might even be a bit more like Indiana Jones: professor by day, tomb raider by night! He would be an expert in the mysteries of our earth and of the universe and would be sought out for his skilled knowledge in various unexplainable phenomena.

Archangel Raziel would most likely feel at home in the countryside of England, away from the hustle and bustle of the city and closer to the magic of nature in the old parts of the country. His house would be simple, but filled with interesting art, unusual artifacts and lots of books. His friends would mostly be made up of colleagues and other experts in science and history and his social life would likely revolve around events at museums, universities, and science centers. He would spend time reading and studying various subjects that revolved around both spirituality and science. He would also spend time simply walking outdoors, feeding birds, and pondering nature. Fascinated with space and the stars, on a clear night, you might find him on a hill with various telescopes. He would seem odd, artistic, old fashioned, quirky, wise, but extremely likable (think of Leonardo Da Vinci). At the end of the day, Archangel Raziel would be pleasantly dozing off with a book in bed with a cold cup of herbal tea, dying candle and smoked pipe on his nightstand.

How You Can Be Like Archangel Raziel

Even though Archangel Raziel is an expert and professor, he didn't get that way by thinking he already knew everything. He is always open to learning more. The scientific method of looking at life allows you to see facts, and understand that facts may change. Being rigid in your thinking doesn't allow you to grow and it makes every relationship in your life more difficult. It's hard to be around people who only see things their way, but it's really fun to be around people who dare to dream, express their imagination and creativity and go with the flow. You can be like Archangel Raziel by being open to new ideas and information. You may not agree with some things, and that is okay. Those concepts and beliefs can float by you like clouds, you do not have to debate or prove anything right or wrong, but just observe things as you would observe clouds passing in the sky.

Archangel Raziel is magic, and so are you! I love telling people that they have magic within them. I love seeing how their face contorts into confusion and then into delight as they consider some sort of inner magician capable of turning dross into gold. There truly is magic within you, and there is magic in the air around you- even now as you read these words. However, magic is tricky; you do not see it unless you believe in it. For the sake of playing with this concept, imagine you are walking out in nature somewhere. Perhaps you live near a forest, desert oasis, lake, river, or ocean. Even a park would do. See yourself walking along and observing all of the things your mind perceives as ultimately possible, such as the trees, the sky, the plants, etc. But what if there was more going on than meets your perception? What if within the trees there were little nature spirits hiding from you, or flying orbs of light above your head, or perhaps talking plants who silenced themselves on your approach? Do you think that perhaps there could be more going on around you than what your logical mind would allow you to take in?

There is a part of you who wants to believe in magical things; this is the magic inside of you. There is a part of you who would love something truly magical to happen in front of you; this is the call from the magic inside of you. There is a part of you who dreams of waving a wand and fixing things in your life, *this* is the magic inside of you. The question isn't whether or not magic exists; the question is when will you consider that this magical side of you exists? If you want to be like Archangel Raziel, you will allow this part of you to emerge and be a part of your everyday life. You will choose to BELIEVE and therefore begin to see miracles and magic all around you. You will no longer fear the mysteries, but embrace them all. You will no longer fear what others think. Be crazy, who cares? Archangel Raziel certainly has no time for the opinions of others, he's too busy being a powerful magician! If you're done with the boring, mundane, monotonous life then let the magic in. Look for it; it is hiding just around the next corner, beneath your pillow, just outside your window....just waiting for you to believe in it so that you can finally see it!

"One comes to believe whatever one repeats to oneself whether the statement be true or false." –Robert Collier

The Mind State

Awareness: First of all, be aware of what you're thinking. Be aware of how your thoughts are making you feel. So many people are numb to negativity because it's their normal trend of thought. But you can't make changes until you choose to really see what is happening. Awareness is everything.

Second, question what you're thinking by asking yourself, "Is that true?" Understand that just because you're hearing it in your head, doesn't make it true. A thought is just a thought, and a thought can be changed. Questioning your thoughts and beliefs is the only sure way to rid yourself of the ones that do not serve what you want out of life. For instance, you may have a belief that something is holding you back. "I need (A) to happen before I do (B)." Is that true? Do you really need something to happen before you can be successful? Or is there something you can do right now, even a small step that would create movement and momentum?

Third, a negative BS comes from fear. You may set yourself up with limiting beliefs because you're afraid of success and happiness, or you don't feel deserving of it. You may even be limiting yourself due to past experiences of hurt or memories of people who wronged you in your life. Fear creates the illusion that you are trapped. You may be holding onto past hurt in an attempt to make sure it doesn't happen again. However, if you understand how life works, holding onto a negative belief will only insure it will happen again and again. Underneath the blame and fear is the path to your success. It's important to be willing to look beyond your fears and ask yourself, "What would I be doing if I wasn't afraid?"

Imagination: Imagination is when creativity meets a thought. If you break down the word itself, you can recognize the word "image". We all have the ability to conjure images in our minds using our imagination. The ability to create an image in our minds is perhaps one of the greatest gifts to the human, as it is the building brick to life. Every castle starts as a castle in the mind. The image within your mind can swiftly be created in the world and this is truly the act of the alchemist who turns nothing into something- non physical into concrete material. If you can see something in your imagination, you have the ability to see it in your world.

Einstein famously said, "Imagination is more important than knowledge. For knowledge is limited to all we now know and understand, while imagination embraces the entire world, and all there ever will be to know and understand." I believe in this statement and have used it to illustrate how when we use our imagination properly, we have the ability to build those castles that begin in our mind.

What happens when we abuse the gift of imagination? Just as we can conjure up pleasant things to create and manifest in our worlds, we also have the ability to misuse our imagination by worrying and imagining the worst possible outcomes. Worry is the abuse of your imagination and if you ever find yourself creating images in your mind that scare you, quickly realize that you are using this gift wrongly, and correct your use of imagination. Stop the fearful images in their tracks and immediately turn them into images you want to see instead. Visualize the happy version of the situation, and use your imagination to conjure up your desires rather than your fears.

Wisdom: Wisdom is quiet. It is still. It is calm. It is also grounded, stable, consistent, and practical. With wisdom, we see life through the eyes of love and understanding. Our fears become insignificant because wisdom lets us see things from a bird's eye perspective. We become less judgmental because wisdom allows us see things from others points of view. We become patient because wisdom tells us that all things come about in their due time.

Wisdom does not mean we know everything. In fact wisdom makes us feel that we have so much more to learn! Wisdom is being teachable and willing to gain more understanding. When we make decisions based on wisdom, we are able to see many options, many outcomes, and many alternatives because we are open, teachable, and excited to discover more. Therefore, wisdom is humility. It is the willingness to lay down our walls and defenses. To admit that the more we learn, the more we realize how little we actually know. In this humble naiveté, we lay down our egoic need to know everything and open ourselves to the wisdom of God.

The Work

Breath is very powerful. You can literally breathe out negativity. You can breathe out your belief that happiness is conditional. You can breathe out the belief that something is standing in your way of success, or that you are trapped. You can breathe out the negative things you think towards yourself and others. Every time a negative thought enters your mind, blow it out. Each night before bed, exhale powerfully and blow the day away. Right now, just do this simple thing: exhale the negativity!

Results can tell you what your true beliefs are, and so can your feelings. Write down the following words and ponder each one for at least 5 minutes to see what kinds of feelings come up for you. For instance, the first word is "Money". How do you really feel about money? Do you feel like money is your friend? What kinds of experiences have you had with money? What do you think about people who have a lot of it? What do you think about people who don't have any? If money was a person in your life, what would your relationship be like? What did your parents teach you about money? What was their attitude? What did you learn from them? What do you wish money would do for you? These are the kinds of questions to ask yourself while paying close attention to how you FEEL, not necessarily what your mind is chattering about.

Each of the following words are topics that people usually have strong beliefs about. Spend some time really looking, saying, and writing each word. You may have to spend more than a few days on this exercise, however investigating your beliefs and feelings is a good way to become aware of any healing, improvement, or changes you might want to make in order to get the results that you are wanting out of life.

Money, partnership, sex, religion, assets, body, health, family, men, women, child, education, animals, self employment, vacation, God, work, nature, home, addiction, silliness, ocean, happiness, success, change, creativity, safety, love, communication, clarity, compassion, growing up, winner, reading, loss, anger, fate, control, exercise, beauty, food, risk, magic, fun, support, authority, lying, technology, confidence, desires.

With all of this investigating and searching, humility is needed when it comes to the things we aren't meant to understand yet.

Remember that you are on a self discovering journey, and some things may not make sense right away. That is okay. Don't stop searching just because you cannot explain something. Put it on the shelf, and continue on. One day, after you have learned more, experienced more, and investigated further, the things on the shelf will be like missing puzzle pieces. Humility in this case means that you are willing to accept the things you cannot change or understand while focusing on the things that you can. Give any and all confusion, weariness, worries, and uncertainty over to God, Archangel Raziel, and to the mystery. Continue learning all you can with what you know right now.

Real Life

When my youngest son, Nick, was 9 years old, he had a problem with a bully in his class. The boy, we'll call "Jake," was very sneaky in the way he mistreated Nick. He would push him at recess but make it look like an accident. He would swat at Nick's lunch, making it fall to the ground and say, "oops," as if he didn't mean it. He would try to get other kids to not play with Nick and my son, who was very sensitive, began hating school because of this boy. The most annoying thing Jake would do was very under the radar. During quiet times in the classroom, Jake would just sit and glare at Nick, shooting energetic daggers at him and making him feel insecure and uncomfortable. Nick, being more of a quiet kid, never went to the teacher because he didn't understand that this was bullying. He believed that bullying was when someone was yelling at you and pushing you around; he had no idea that this sort of sideways, sneaky assault was in fact a form of bullying. When Nick finally came to me about what was going on at school, you can imagine I found myself caught between wanting to march into the class and strangle the kid and wanting to use this as a learning tool to teach Nick how to deal with difficult people and bullies. I chose the latter, knowing that this would probably not be the last time Nick would have to deal with someone like this and instead of fighting his battle, I opted to give him his own armor. I contacted the teacher and he said he was aware Jake was causing some trouble, but that he didn't realize to what extent. I told the teacher that my intention was to help Nick deal with this kid on his own first and the teacher agreed to stand aside, keep a watchful eye, intervene when necessary, and allow Nick to stand up for himself.

The first thing we focused on was Nick's own beliefs about being a victim. I showed Nick a picture of a warrior and then of a victim and asked him which one he identified with. With much emotion in his face, he pointed to the victim but then quickly stated that he really wanted to be the warrior.

The second thing we discussed was how just like Nick's belief that he was a victim was showing up in his life, Jakes inner beliefs were showing up too. I told him that bullies are really just scared, insecure, and jealous people who want to cover up their true emotions by being scary. Nick admitted that he thought Jake might be jealous of him because Nick was so likeable and funny, and Jake was not. In not only investigating Nick's beliefs to uncover why he was a target for Jake, but investigating Jake's own results, we were able to pinpoint what his beliefs were too. One boy was jealous and filled with insecurity, the other felt like he was a victim. It was a perfect match for the results that were showing up for them both. Nick understood that by changing his beliefs from being the victim to being a warrior, he would be able to change his results with Jake.

I began to ask Nick "What if" questions like: What would you do if you were a warrior? How would "warrior Nick" act around Jake? This got Nick thinking outside of the victim box and opened him up to all kinds of possibilities. Some of them were funny, like warrior Nick would accuse Jake of being in love with him because he stared at him during class all day. Some of them were insightful like, warrior Nick would learn from Jake how *not* to treat other people, even if you are jealous of them. Warrior Nick would stand up to Jake, expose him for the bully he was instead of continuing to let it go under the radar. Warrior Nick would never let Jake see that he was affecting him; he would be stronger than Jake.

We discussed why Nick felt that he was a victim, and by bringing some very deep seated issues to the surface, Nick was no longer at the whim to these unconscious beliefs. He was able to choose something else for himself. I knew that as my son healed the reasons he felt like a victim to life, that his results would change, and I was thankful we were addressing this so young in his life. Even though we may have an absolute perfect reason and justification for being a victim, the mentality behind it only creates more situations where we are victimized.

My son had lost his father two years prior to this bully incident. Was he a victim? Yes. Did I choose to raise him as one? No. Nick had to face the most horrible thing any child has to face, the death of a beloved parent. He has every reason to think and behave like a victim, and to be honest most of society would support that. Most people, with good intentions, would excuse Nick's meekness and support him being a victim for the rest of his life because of his tragedy. But after our conversation, my son and I agreed that being a victim just didn't fit. Every tragedy offers us a choice. Fear takes away the free agency to choose between becoming stronger, or becoming weaker by telling us that we are now a victim for the rest of our lives. Moving fear aside for Nick meant that he could now choose to become stronger. Nick's daddy would have wanted Nick to be "Warrior Nick," not a victim. And so the warrior training began!

We practiced role playing where I was Jake, and Nick was Warrior Nick. This allowed Nick to see that he was powerful in all sorts of different circumstances. I asked Nick to use his imagination to visualize himself standing up to all bullies with fairness and strength. I could see his thought process change from shyly cowering away to standing powerfully and responding with a calm strength that would intimidate anyone who wanted to push him around. We pretended to put on an invisible armor and by the time I dropped Nick off at school, I had no doubt that he was ready to show the world that he had changed. He had made the choice to become something else and perhaps changed the entire course of his life. I watched my son walk into the building with his shoulders back and head held high. He was Warrior Nick.

I arrived to pick him up from school early. Even though I had played it strong with Nick, I was nervous for him. I knew that this was a big deal, and that Nick needed to set the stage for how he would allow others to treat him. I eagerly caught his eye as he bounced along the school's sidewalk and into the car. He was adorned with the biggest and brightest warrior grin I had ever seen. Calmly I asked, "So? How was your day?"

Nick recounted his experience standing up to Jake. It was during quiet reading time that Nick caught him glaring at him as usual. Nick said he finally slammed his book down and loudly asked, "Jake, how come you just stare at me all day. Like, are you in love with me or something?" At that the entire room burst out into a roaring laugh. The other kids jumped in agreement and saying things like, "Ya Jake, I catch you staring at Nick all the time and it bugs me, why do you do that?" Nick said that his teacher did not break up the interruption, but that he also joined the inquiry. This exposure sent a very strong message to the now embarrassed little sneak- that he wouldn't be able to get away with it any longer.

Ever since that incident, Nick has carried himself differently. He knows that he's not a victim, and I have no doubt that his new belief will give him new results. Nick saw it in his imagination first; he prepared himself, and then carried forth his desire to be stronger like a true warrior. As for Jake, by the end of the year, he and Nick became friends! I don't think Warrior Nick will have that problem again.

Archangel Raziel's Message To The Modern World: *"The only thing that holds you back is your own limiting beliefs. It is an illusion to believe that anything outside of you can have the power to stop you, for it is you who has given anything on the outside the power to hinder you. It is imperative and of timely essence that you begin to investigate all of your limitations, like an open minded, non-judging scientist investigating a theory. Of all of the work you will do in your life, this will be the most important and beneficial. We angels need you to be strong and free from your self imposed chains so that you can rise with us to heal the entire world. You. Are. Limitless. Believe this, believe in yourself, and nothing can stop you."*

Questions To Consider: Are you willing to take a look at what you truly believe about yourself and the world around you? Are you ready to take your power back from the illusion of obstacles? Can you practice humility and trust the mystery of life and accept that not everything has to be explained and understood? What is the one belief that you have that stands in your way? These are the questions to consider if you want to be like the open minded, wise, and mysterious Archangel Raziel.

Chapter 13

Archangel Sandalphon- The Hippie

Chill Bro

"I'm here!" She whispered her announcement. It wasn't for anyone in particular, just a statement to the elements that she had arrived. Taking in a deep breath, she felt the salt from the sea air travel up into her mind, down into her heart and lungs, clearing away the pollution and fog. She pushed her feet further into the sand and felt for the first time in ages what it was like to feel truly grounded to the earth. The waves seemed to be applauding her private homecoming, beckoning her to play. Dropping everything, she gracefully glided through the sand until the waves kissed her toes bringing delight to her face. "I'm here." She whispered excitedly again to the ocean. She could already sense herself changing as she moved forward into the inviting waves. The crashing sound began to break through her shell, opening her up. Her heart began to race as she swam further out past the breaking waves and into an eternal world she had almost forgotten. The salt of her tears, the salt of the sea, she was coming undone and coming together all at once. Her hair was wild in the water, her skin sparkling in the sunlight. She was breath, heart, lungs, and joy. "You're here" the ocean whispered back taking her into its belly once more.

Archangel Sandalphon is the second Archangel whose name does not end in 'el'. Like Archangel Metatron, it is said that at one time Archangel Sandalphon was human- and to be specific he was the prophet Elijah. In the Books of Kings Elijah had been travelling for 40 days and nights for a spiritual purpose when he takes shelter in the cave on Mount

151

Horeb for the night. Upon awakening, he is visited by God. This goes to show that when you finally stop, chill, and rest, you receive the epiphany you've been working so hard to get. And that is the essence of Archangel Sandalphon; slow down. It is within a rested mind that great insight can take place.

Have you ever had the experience of going on a vacation and after you have been away from the mundane work filled life you come home with all of these new ideas and motivation to make positive changes? It's always on the way home from being out of the trees that we are able to see the forest and therefore gain a better perspective of things. We seem less attached to things when we are above it looking down, we feel more peace when the larger picture is presented. Little things that we became attached to and obsessed with seem small and petty as the bigger meaning is revealed. This is why it is so important to take time away and out of your life. Ideally, it is best to do this every day. Even for 20 minutes, to just go sit somewhere quiet and lovely and just CHILL. Like a computer, when we run too many programs at once, we become slow and tired. Taking time out is like clicking 'close' on thoughts, stresses, projects and this allows us to reboot.

I'm going to admit here that I do indeed, on occasion, say the F word... and I like it. The way I see it, it's just a word; some letters put together to form a sound. It is your perception of the word that makes it bad. However, my perception of the word has changed. I have decided that it feels really good to say sometimes. And let's face it, certain stories and jokes just aren't the same without it. Through times of stress, chaos, pain, and drama, a funny and personal acronym has been formed: CTFO which stands for Chill The Fuck Out. I am unapologetically admitting that there are times when CTFO is the only thing that realigns me, centers and grounds me, and gets me to calm down enough to be clear in my mind and heart again. I am impenitently telling the world that I have been known to climb a mountain in the pouring rain just to be completely alone so that I could invoke the word FUCK as loud and as many times as I could until the tears, breakthrough, and pending calm came for me. Why am I talking about this vulgar word in my book of angelic advice? Because Archangel Sandalphon is the absolute epitome of chilling the fuck out about things, and if there is one thing I've learned from this powerful being, it's that we stress and freak out over things that are frightfully small compared to the whole of all things. Archangel Sandalphon literally represents the bird's eye (or angel's eye) view of life and reminds us of a bigger picture. He tells us that if we can just chill out and relax, things will be okay. The relief and liberation that the F word brings in times of extreme stress is amazing, and I invite you to put away your little perceptions and use my acronym next time it is needed. Alone in your car where no one can hear you, just yell it to yourself, CHILL THE FUCK OUT ALREADY! You'll thank me later.

If Archangel Sandalphon were human I am convinced he'd be a hippie. Long dreadlocks, tan skin, attending weekly drum circles with his hemp backpack filled with organic fruit and nuts hanging off of his eco-friendly earth bike. He'd spend his morning sun saluting on the sand before surfing- invigorating and inviting the elements and his breath to wake his body into a new beautiful, stress free, glorious day. He would live simply, happily finding the joys in the little things. Everywhere he would go, people would know him and wave. He would be friendly and very likable- always being the one to hold doors open, help a stranger, give to the poor, and constantly making people laugh. Being caring, innovative, and good with his hands, he would make money by helping people with odd jobs as a mechanic, maintenance, and handyman. His life would be like being on a vacation; he would own just enough and work just enough to be comfortable and happy. He would take pride in a few treasures, mostly wonderful memories and friendships. Life would be kind to him, as he would be kind to others and the only people who would judge him would be the people who secretly longed for his carefree bright and happy life by the sea.

Archangel Sandalphon would live in a small but quaint shack-like house that would be clean, organized, and simple with beach towels drying on chairs outside by his surfboard. He would live very close to the beach, if not right on it. He would be musically inclined and own a ukulele and perhaps some drums and people would love to hear him sing songs around a beach fire at sunset. At the end of the day, Sandalphon would feel fulfilled, appreciated, surrounded by good friends, and ultimately satisfied. He would feel that even though he wasn't making huge waves in the world, that more often than not, it's just being kind to those around you that make the biggest difference.

How You Can Be Like Archangel Sandalphon

Archangel Sandalphon not only teaches us how to chill out about things, but he also wishes us to know that happiness comes from understanding and applying the "ripple effect". When you understand that even the smallest gesture of kindness and positivity can ripple out from you and affect millions, you will begin to participate in them daily, without judgment of how your influence on the world has to look. I believe that on some level everyone wants to make a difference. Everyone wants to send out ripples of their goodness into the world, yet far too often we find ourselves in the midst of negative ripples instead.

Think of a negative ripple effect. Maybe you had a bad experience in a store and not only did you never go back, but you told everyone about the bad service. Think about if you had a negative interaction with someone: this could put them in a negative mood so that they treat someone else the way you treated them, and that person in turn treats another poorly. One interaction went wrong and negative ripples were sent out in all directions, affecting more people than you can imagine. But if this is not what we truly want to happen in our world, why do we continue causing these ripples?

We are unconscious of the power of the ripple effect. We might "get it", (oh ya, Crystal wrote a cute piece about how we affect the world around us, so nice...) but we don't truly understand it because if we did, we would begin to understand with urgency the importance of stopping negative ripples in their tracks.

You have to be in control of the ripples you produce. It is called the ripple effect because like a stone being cast into water, eventually those ripples will reach a rebound point and come back to you. The stronger the waves you send out into the world the more momentum they will have when they hit their rebound point, and guess what that means for you? Have you ever caught yourself saying, "Man, bad luck just comes at me in waves!" Perhaps you sent out bad ripples and now here they are, back to get you.

Successful people aren't happy because they are successful; they were happy first. They sent out the right ripples. On some level they were aware of the ripple effect, and they used it to their advantage.

To be like Archangel Sandalphon, you need to understand that it's all about the little things like:

- Shaking the hand of the person bagging your groceries.
- Letting someone in front of you in a line.
- Opening the door and actually smiling at someone.
- Having compassion for the overworked and underpaid waitress, customer service rep, ticket taker, and others in service jobs and leaving a generous tip and compliment.
- Speaking to the manager of a store and taking time to work out a win-win solution to a problem so that you can give a good review later.
- Spending time with an animal or child who needs attention and love.
- Telling the person at the drive through to put your change towards the car's order in back of you.
- Stopping to help someone change a tire.
- Smiling patiently at a publically screaming baby and her sleep deprived mother.
- Texting a friend or loved one randomly to tell them how much they mean to you.
- Lightening up a stressful situation with a cheerful comment or joke.
- Actively listening to someone who is having a hard time explaining their point of view with the intention to help them feel understood.
- Surrounding yourself with positive people who also put out happy ripples.
- Consciously deciding you will not be a part of a negative ripple effect.
- And finally, my favorite small but powerful ripple- Simply pray. Send someone a well wish, good vibes, whatever you do to pour your love into them. I believe that the strongest ripples are the ones that come from your heart. You never know how those ripples will expand and change your entire world. One day you'll wake up and feel the rebound of that love and wonder how life got so good!

"To have faith is to trust yourself to the water. When you swim you don't grab hold of the water, because if you do you will sink and drown. Instead you relax, and float."-Alan Watts

The Mind State

Detachment: The more attached you are to an outcome, the less power you have. If you think that a circumstance, person, or a thing can bring you your happiness, you are setting yourself up in a situation where you are powerless. Let's take relationships for example. You find someone who makes you happy, and you immediately become attached to the expectation that they will always make you happy. Then, when you inevitably find out they are a human being- imperfect, fallible, weak, here to make mistakes and learn- you are overly disappointed by their failure to meet your expectations. Because of their natural faults, all your hopes for happiness are now gone. We give relationships so much power that when it goes through a rough time, your ultimate happiness is threatened. But, the moment you release other people from the responsibility of being your source of happiness, you will come to understand that true happiness comes from YOU. You will be able to find joy and peace regardless of what your partner is doing or not doing. Whenever you depend on anything other than your own inner light to bring you happiness, you become insecure, weak, and co-dependent.

Detachment requires you to get comfortable with the unexpected. Life is filled with uncertainty and the more risks you take, the higher the likelihood for uncertain outcomes will be. You have to be flexible. Imagine how confident and happy you would be if you embraced the fact that the only certainty in life is change, and were able to take in stride every change that came your way. People who attach themselves to particular, finite outcomes are shocked and find themselves stuck when life brings unexpected surprises. They are prepared for one outcome and one outcome only, and are often unable to adapt if events follow a different course than the one they had planned for. Rigid thinking can and will literally paralyze you. Be unwavering about your goal, but flexible in your methods getting there. Your willingness to change your mind in order to go with the flow is the only way to keep from being thrown off your course completely when the unexpected comes your way. Anyone who has accomplished anything will tell you that it never turns out the way they planned- but more often than not, it turns out better!

Serenity: I can't hear this word without hearing George Costanza's father on the popular TV Series "Jerry Seinfeld," yelling, "Serenity Now!" That might date me, but those of you who grew up with Seinfeld will appreciate the reference, as I'm sure we've all had days where we want to just yell to the sky, "Serenity Now!!"

Serenity is like a calm, clear lake; beautiful and peaceful. When life becomes chaotic, we yearn for serenity and some sort of stillness within the storm. When you feel serene, you feel like nothing or no one can bother or upset you. You are dedicated and unwavering to your peace of mind, and unlike the extremely stressed out father on Seinfeld, you radiate a calm demeanor of faith and trust that all is well in your world.

Anytime you achieve serenity, you still the waters of your mind and you are able to clearly see yourself, your situations, your relationships, and your connection to your Creator. It is easy to feel that all of your questions are answered, and that you are being divinely guided in your life. Practicing being serene is important, and if you happen to be having a flustering day, don't be afraid to declare, "Serenity Now!" and breathe until you reach that place for you.

Laughter: Think about the last time you had a really deep and out of control belly laugh, the kind of laughter that pulls you out of your body, where you are almost watching yourself lose control in hysteria. Has it been a while? If so, what are you going to do about that? Here's the truth about laughter: the reason it's so important is because your ego (the part of you that doubts, worries, fears, and talks you out of being an amazing earth angel) doesn't know what to do when you are deep in laughter. It literally has nothing to say about it. Therefore, you are the furthest away from your ego's influence when your walls are down, and you are crazy laughing your guts out. Laughter shakes out the fear and leaves you feeling happier, clearer, and more relaxed. When you are relaxed and open to laughter, it is so much easier for your angels to whisper new insights and suggestions to you. You are naturally more connected to your Creator because all of your defenses and fears have been laughed aside. Having a regular dose of laughter can keep you open to new ideas, solutions, and creativity. Perhaps this is why some of the most enlightened and creative people in the world are also the first to laugh at anything. They take themselves and things lightly, and in doing so, they remain open to possibilities. Perhaps this is why we call laughter the best medicine on the world!

How can you be easier to laugh? I am sure you can think of some things to laugh about in yourself and others. Of course, I caution you here that you never laugh at yourself or others in a cruel way, or to make fun of something. I'm talking about the kind of laughter that feels like sunshine that lights up our mind and heart. Think of being merry, joyous, jolly, and fun. Think about the laughing Buddha; he certainly knew how to have a good time with his enlightenment, and there is truth in his quote, *"When you realize how perfect everything is, you will tilt your head back and laugh at the sky."*

The Work

Who and what do you depend to give you happiness? Really be honest with yourself and become aware of who or what you have given your power away to by making it a source of your happiness. If your spouse, religion, team, best friend, child, mentor, or job were to change- how deeply would you be affected? In what situations do you have major expectations for the outcome? It's time to detach! Write down the three greatest expectations you have for the people in your life and ask yourself if you are being fair to them. Perhaps you have given them more responsibility over your happiness than you've meant to.

Write down situations that stress you out and how you can become more flexible in your thinking. In other words, what areas of your life do you just need to CTFO? When we let go of our fixed expectations, we open ourselves up to even better outcomes. Whenever I think of an outcome I really want, I usually think to myself, "This or something better!" This helps me be open to possibilities.

Archangel Sandalphon is a simple guy. He's not into complicating his life with a bunch of meaningless possessions, and since he understands that happiness doesn't come from "things", the items he does own have meaning and purpose to him. Very often we search for happiness in the next big thing we can buy or indulge in, thinking it will satisfy us or bring us our next level of joy. Then we complain that we can't take care or use everything we have. All of our gadgets, devices, electronics, and recreational items begin to take up room, collect dust, and complicate our lives. Because we think all of these possessions will bring us true happiness, we get upset when they don't live up to such expectations. Then we buy more stuff and before we know it, our lives are jam-packed with an excess of *things*. Archangel Sandalphon is here to teach us that by removing pointless possessions from our lives we create the uninterrupted joy and happiness we were seeking when we bought all of those things. Letting go of much gives you much.

In what ways can you begin to simplify your life? Perhaps it's time to get rid of household items you rarely or never use. This will create space in your surroundings and help you to feel less burdened and responsible over too many things. You'll feel free, clear, and liberated as you work to simplify your life!

Real Life

I was pregnant with my youngest son when I found myself at the Fellowship Gardens in Encinitas, California. It was a place where I found much solace and peace each time I visited, and on this particular visit I was seeking some serenity. After winding through pathways of lush tropical trees and flowers and playing with Koi fish in a pond, I found a bench on the top of the bluff overlooking the vast blue Pacific Ocean. Taking in a deep breath, I began to pray about things that worried me. My marriage was falling apart but I wasn't brave enough to talk to anyone about it. I wasn't making very good money and felt there was no way out. I was worried about my unborn baby, and I was worried about my older son. I felt so lost and alone and while breathing in the clean salt air and tropical trees, I prayed for answers. In my mind's eye, I had a vision of a man dressed in white. He simply said to me, "Detach from drama and know that all is well."

When I opened my eyes, I felt like a huge weight had been lifted off of my shoulders. I realized that my stress came from an unhealthy attachment to how I wanted things to be. I wondered if it was possible to be too attached to my children and husband, and I realized how controlling I had become over the people in my life. It was the first time I had learned about co-dependency and how my unhealthy attachments to people, situations, my past, and expectations were ruining my life.

My prayer shifted from "God please save me," to "God, please help me to detach from drama and believe that all is well." As I began to unravel myself from unhealthy relationships and my need to control everyone and everything around me, I learned how to chill out, let go and trust the process of life.

Archangel Sandalphon's Message To The Modern World: *"Stress will never help you to create an ideal outcome. You can take stress out of a situation, or not- and the situation will not change. However, your reaction and decisions will inevitably differ depending on whether you have allowed stress to be a part of the solution process or not. Many of you believe that you work better under stress. Perhaps stress propels you to complete a task, but the quality of work will not be as great as if would have completed it in a calm manner. The idea that stress is good in any way is a complete lie and a sure way to sabotage your health, clarity, success, and peace of mind. You must learn how to let go of your strict expectations, and detach from your ideal outcome if you really want what is best for everyone involved. You will be delightfully surprised at how easy things really can be, and how powerful you are not only for yourself but for others when you learn how to simply CHILL."*

Questions To Consider: What kind of ripple effect are you creating in your world? In what ways are you strict with yourself and others? When was the last time you took a vacation? Do you make time to regularly relax, meditate, or engage in peaceful things like sitting in nature, getting massage, or taking a yoga class? How might you judge those who decide to live a simple and stress free life? What can you do today to make a peaceful difference in your life? In what ways are you too controlling? These are things to think about if you want to be easy going, happy, funny, and as cool as the breeze in the trees Archangel Sandalphon.

Chapter 14

Archangel Uriel- The Prophet

The Best Way To Predict The Future Is To Create It

He was ready for her. It had taken him longer than he had expected; to heal the wounds that bled anger and betrayal from his heart. But that was a long time ago. Now, he was ready for her. He had room for her clothing in his closet. He had a space for her in his bed. He had all of her favorite things to enjoy. Trips planned, words to be spoken, memories to be made, he was ready for her... And wondered who she might be.

Archangel Uriel is best known for his role in the Bible as the angel who boldly warned Noah of the pending flood, and told him to prepare by building the ark. Just as he did for Noah, Archangel Uriel delivers prophetic information to us and tells us how to be prepared.

His name means "God's Light." Everything about Archangel Uriel is bright and illuminating. He helps us to see clearly through darkness, and urges us to prepare for our future by creating what we want in the present moment. He says that we cannot create solutions to our problems with the same mentality and mind state that created the problem. We must be willing to change what we are doing and prepare to receive the blessings we have asked for.

I always imagine Archangel Uriel holding a lantern and illuminating a staircase, guiding us upward one step at a time. Often times in our lives it's hard to see every single step towards a goal, but the important thing is that we take the next step when it appears. Many people remain stuck at the bottom of their staircase because they need to see the entire plan before ascending. That first step of any climb is making the decision to have faith, and trust that the next step will reveal itself as you move towards your goal. I've talked to many successful people who admit they had no idea what the exact steps toward their goals would be, but they were willing to take each one as they revealed themselves. Archangel Uriel teaches us to trust our inner knowing, have faith that the steps are there, prepare for anything, and jump in!

Because of Archangel Uriel's prophetic warning to Noah regarding the impending storm, Archangel Uriel is associated with weather patterns. This is also reflected in his personality and the way he communicates. Archangel Uriel is like a lightning bolt, bright, bold, and to the point and his presence can lead us to have epiphanies and deep insight.

Currently, our modern day lifestyle isn't dependant on or much affected by the weather. We have secure homes and buildings where we can control the thermostat. We also get year-round food delivered from our local grocery stores therefore the turn of the seasons and the agricultural cycles do not affect us like it did our ancestors. However, there was a time when we all paid very close attention to the weather and the seasonal wheel. We had a very respectful relationship to nature because we literally depended on it to live. The separation between man and nature was inevitable within our evolution and growth. However, there will always be a part of us that longs to reconnect to the abundance, joy, beauty, bounty, timing and rhythms of the planet. Archangel Uriel can help us to remember how to stay grounded and connected to the earth. He asks us to get outside and experience our world outside of our homes and computers. Archangel Uriel loves it when we take time to notice the sunset, rest under a tree, to dance in the rain, and to play in the snow.

Archangel Uriel, if he were human, would embrace this inner call to be wild and free like a brewing storm. He would be a force to be reckoned with and anything he put his attention onto would be faced with a downpour of hard work and determination. Like the forces of nature, Archangel Uriel would have several sides to his personality and his interests would be vast. However due to his prophetic nature, he would always seem to be one step ahead of the world. He would first and foremost be an entrepreneur and an extremely respected and revered business man. He would dig into business endeavors like a farmer digs crops. He would know the right time to begin or invest in a business, grow his business, harvest the fruits of his labors, and of course he would be happy to share his bounty with those around him. Archangel Uriel would also know when to sell a business and move onto the next project. Like the weather patterns, always flowing from one deal to the next, making a huge difference, and then rolling into the next one. He would blow through one step at a time, tactfully and deliberately. He would be a well known and sought after business mentor helping many entrepreneurs reach success.

However, another side to Archangel Uriel would be a deep fascination with astrology. He would perhaps even study it with the intentions of learning when astrologically it is best to start businesses, sell, or prepare for a downfall. There is a lot that astrology can tell us. Whether you want to believe or not, the planets and their position affect our world, and affect our lives. Our ancestors not only studied weather patterns and seasons, but they also relied on the stars as a clock to tell them when the best time to grow and cultivate crops would be. I think that Archangel Uriel would find it worth his while to look into the birth charts of those he would do business with to see if they would astrologically mesh with his plans. His personality would not care if his serious study of astrology seemed quirky or unconventional- Archangel Uriel would be his own man, owing nothing to anyone.

Archangel Uriel would live in a very large and lush house and drive an expensive fast car with a license plate that simply said, "Trust." To him trust means that if you want to create your future, you must trust yourself, your gut, the process, your work, and what you have done to prepare. Then trust that you will how to climb the staircase.

Archangel Uriel would not look anything like the prophets of old; he would be clean shaven, dress classy, and sport the latest watch and shoes. One might consider him to be a wealthy modern day spiritualist. With all of his committed and serious actions, there would definitely be a wild side to this man. Not careless or immature by any means, he would embody an untamed power adorned by the abundance his unbridled drive pursued. Archangel Uriel would be a very committed lover, as committed as a storm cloud is to showering the earth. He would spoil his sweetheart with affection, attention, and all of the good things he would provide. The woman who stood by this dynamic man would be a beautiful balance. She would be like sunshine to his thunderous "go for it" attitude, and offer him soft love and gentle tenderness. Together they would travel, play, celebrate success, and work to better themselves in all areas of their lives. At the end of the day, Archangel Uriel would feel satisfied, solid, and accomplished. You might find him sitting at the edge of his pool with his wife watching the sun set and appreciating the natural view.

How You Can Be Like Archangel Uriel

If you want to be like Archangel Uriel, you need to engage your own inner storm and be unafraid of the effects of the whirlwind your success might create! Of course, you will have to prepare for such a bold move. Build your ark. Build your empire. Get your hands dirty and line your crops. Be strategic and straightforward. Then unleash your true nature and watch your life grow and bloom like wild crops!

Archangel Uriel is a powerful communicator, so be bold, straight up, and 100% honest with the people around you, even if you are afraid of their reactions to your honesty. Archangel Uriel doesn't have time to baby everyone around him and make sure that everyone is okay with him. He also knows that by being honest about his feelings and thoughts, that no one is left guessing or hanging on to assumptions. One of the best things you can do to be like Archangel Uriel is to let people know where you are in any given situation, relationship, and issue. Even if your authenticity makes them feel uncomfortable, remember that it is not in your power to control others reactions. Every time you have been inauthentic, you have kept someone else from making a fully informed and potentially better choice for themselves. For instance, if Archangel Uriel felt that a certain person wasn't a good fit for a project, instead of keeping them on board to save feelings, he would be upfront and honest with them. He would know that by holding someone hostage in a situation they are not 100% fit for, he would be filling the space for someone who is a better fit while at the same time keeping the first person from being in a position that is better for them.

In a relationship scenario, by staying with someone you are not 100% committed to because you are afraid of hurting their feelings, you are keeping them from being with someone who will love them and who is a better fit for them. If you want to be like Archangel Uriel, let people know where you are, how you're feeling, and what you're thinking at appropriate times so that they have an opportunity to react and reassess.

You can also be like Archangel Uriel by practicing forward thinking and by making plans. I imagine Archangel Uriel would be the kind of entrepreneur who would run numbers, statics, and he would keep score of how his goals were coming along. Write out the steps you know you need to take, and track your progress. We've talked a lot about how to deal with the past. Archangel Uriel, as the prophetic type of Archangel, would help you to look forward and realize that you are creating your future by what you are doing right now.

"I advise you to say your dream is possible and then overcome all inconveniences, ignore all the hassles and take a running leap through the hoop, even if it is in flames."-Les Brown

The Mind State

Opportunity: You can change your entire life by taking a step in the direction of where you want to be right now, but you may have a barrier in your way. What is blocking your ability to take the next step? Do you believe you need to have more money? Are you afraid to do it alone? Do you believe you have to look a certain way or be more qualified? I want you to begin to see your barriers as delay tactics that you have set up for yourself due to fear. Opportunities can only be taken advantage of by those who are prepared and are already taking the steps necessary for success. By preparation, I mean that you have addressed your delay tactics (fears) so that when the opportunity arrives, you are able to take action with no hesitation. You must prepare yourself everyday by overcoming whatever stands in the way of you and your success. Do not delay- get ready and be prepared so that you will take opportunities when they come.

Expectancy: Very often when you are taking that first step into the unknown, your enthusiasm can be squelched when your mind gets in the way and begins telling you all of the reasons it won't work out. Limiting thoughts- like you don't have the resources, people, money- and feelings of frustration, doubt, and fear rise to the surface and you feel stuck on step one. Recognize that all those thoughts and emotions are your unhealthy resistance to your success due to fear. If there's anything Archangel Uriel can teach us, it's the ability to rise above the resistance. You must realize that your inner naysayer is designed to make you fail, and once you see resistance for what it really is, you can begin ignoring it. Like Archangel Uriel showing the way with his lantern, illuminate your way with this powerful word- EXPECTANCY. When you absolutely expect for things to work out, line up, and manifest you are rising up above the resistance that is telling you otherwise. It has been proven that people who expect to see good things in their lives will inevitably see more good things happen for them. When you embody the truth that your outcome will work out perfectly no matter what, you attract exactly what the resistance is saying you don't have. So, every time the resistance to your journey rises, ignore it with the confidence that you absolutely 100% expect the best to happen.

Generosity: When you are feeling sure about yourself and your future, it is easy to be generous with others. Generosity is an attitude that says you are more than happy to give without expecting anything in return. This is easy to do when you recognize your own abundance. No matter what you have right now in your life, you are able to tap into an ever-flowing source of abundance. This abundance isn't just wealth, but it is also health, breath, life, energy, love, happiness, and joy. When you notice how abundant you can feel at any given moment just by tapping into this source of abundance, you are ready to give of yourself freely, openly, and lovingly. There is no lack; there is always something you can give. You can give a prayer, a smile, a flower, a helping hand. And you can also give money, food, and gifts. The rewards for being generous are infinite because what you give is always returned to you multiplied.

Gratitude: Whenever you are thankful for something, you get more of it. Gratitude is literally THE medicine for all discord. Feel sad? Think about what you're grateful for. Feel lost? Think about what you're grateful for. Feel sick? Think about what you're grateful for. Lost your job? Think about what you're grateful for. You get the picture. I can guarantee that counting your blessings will bestow upon you a better mood, and open your eyes to notice more things to be grateful for.

When we are truly feeling grateful, we can't help but to show it! Archangel Uriel teaches us that when we show gratitude to the world, we spread joy and the world gives back to us more to be grateful for. Since gratitude is such a contagious feeling, when we show gratitude to those around us, we give them the opportunity to feel thankful too! Sharing our gratitude with others is also a very powerful medicine. I have witnessed the healing of relationships, health, and financial crisis with healthy doses of gratitude. When you say, "Thank you," you are sending a powerful signal to yourself, others, and to the angels that you are happy, joyful, blessed, and ready for more!

Gratitude is the key to opening doors to universal abundance. If there is one thing that you take away from this section, or perhaps the entire book that will make the greatest difference in your mind state, it is to just be grateful. Every day! As often as you can! Cultivate an attitude of gratitude and you will open yourself up to receive love and abundance into your life as you've never imagined!

The Work

Write down two specific things you are willing to try right now that are out of your comfort zone. The first thing should be something you've never tried before. The second thing should be something you've tried and failed at. Commit right now to trying again. Take the first steps. You don't have to know what you're doing after the first step, just take it and see what happens!

Create a ritual. Even with his wild nature, Archangel Uriel would be a man of consistency. Consistency has been proven to instill a sense of safety and security in a chaotic world. You might create some sort of night-time ritual where you consistently meditate, read, work on tomorrow's plan and to-do list, or you might have a weekly nature walk. Perhaps you want the consistency of a date night or family time. Whatever it is that you are working on to improve, you must become ritualistic about it. When my kids were young, they sometimes found bedtime hard. So, I taught my children my beautiful nighttime ritual that helps us all begin to shut down and sleep better. An hour before bedtime, all screens are turned off (TV, computers, games, tablets, phones, etc) I begin to dim lights, I infuse lavender or incense in the air, and we begin to calm our minds and bodies. We read, talk and connect to each other, stretch or do some gentle yoga, take a bath, drink calming tea, and do things that purposely and gently lead us into bedtime. By the time our heads hit the pillow, we have worked out the over-stimulation of the day, we've spent time together, and we are ready for sleep. This one simple nightly ritual can change your life, especially if you have a hard time falling asleep.

Astrology can be a powerful tool, one that everyone can benefit from studying. Like the kind of person Archangel Uriel would be, consider finding out how your own planets affect you. Even if you take it with a grain of salt, looking up your birth chart, or having a professional astrologer give you a birth chart reading can help you when it comes to the timing of your life. Think of your astrology chart like a giant clock. There really are times in your life when it's best to get married, have children, start businesses, quit jobs, travel, buy, sell, etc. It's not like we are held tightly to these influences, however you'll find that knowing your birth chart and planets can help you make decisions and plan for the easiest and most successful outcomes. After all, astrology is certainly nothing new. It is how the Magi found Jesus. It's a time proven strategy that can put you ahead of the game so many ways!

Who and what needs your appreciation right now? Archangel Uriel knows that whenever you show someone appreciation, they tend to work even harder. Whenever you show God and the angels appreciation, more good comes to you. By showing appreciation for everything and everyone around you, you are actually empowering your environment and surroundings. You'll see people work even more efficiently, and you'll feel waves of good things coming back to you.

Real Life

The following story is of a moment where I believe I changed the outcome of my entire life. It is the moment I decided to think outside of a very small box in which I was living, and create a better future for myself.

I took the first step out of poverty when I only had two dollars left to my name. As a very young single mother who hardly had enough money to pay bills, I found myself one day walking with my son to get food from the dollar menu at McDonalds with the last two dollars I had. It was a nice day, I remember feeling the warmth of the sun on my face, and hearing my son giggle as we made a silly game of dodging the cracks on the sidewalk on our way. I also remember the heaviness of my heart as I wondered how we would eat tomorrow. I knew I had a "lack mentality" problem, and that it was indeed my belief system and mind state that had ultimately gotten me into this position. I wanted to change my life, but I had no idea what step to take. Halfway to the McDonalds, we passed a man sitting on the corner with a sign begging for money. I looked at him and thought to myself, "If I had more money, I would give a dollar to this man." I felt bad that I couldn't help him, until I had another thought. "I don't like feeling so poor! I want to feel rich, and I want to believe I am rich!" So I took a powerful action step and gave the man half of everything I had; a whole dollar. He was so thankful, and it really felt good to give. I suddenly felt powerful and abundant! I felt peaceful as I watched my son eat his meager dinner. I realized then and there that I wanted to feel successful and wealthy more than I wanted to eat!

Even though I had no idea what to do next, I knew I had taken the first step. The miracle isn't what happened next, although as you read about it you may think that it was the miracle. I want to be clear that to me, the miracle was my change of attitude towards my finances and willingness to feel limitless. The miracle was the moment I decided to practice my free agency and chose how to react to circumstance rather than be a victim to it. What happened next was a result of that miracle that took place within me.

When I woke up the next morning, my stomach was hungry and I found myself in a mental war between my new ideas of feeling limitless and stressing about what we would eat. My son wasn't awake yet and so I decided to open the front door of our very tiny one-bedroom apartment and get some fresh air to think. When I opened the door, I couldn't believe what I saw! On my doorstep, someone had placed several grocery bags filled with food! I was completely taken aback and in awe! I remember feeling relieved, humbled, grateful, and so many other emotions as I went through the bags. There might as well have been a million dollars sitting in my kitchen when I finally put everything away. I knew that somehow, by changing my belief in being limited by my lack of money, and taking the first step towards being an abundant person, that I had somehow created a much different scenario for my future! Somebody out there was taking action too- whoever took the time to buy us food and mysteriously leave it on my doorstep was taking steps they were guided to take, and everything was coming together because we were all taking action!

To this day, I have no idea who that person was, but I thank them for listening to their own personal guidance, because it was a very powerful sign to me and it changed my life. I've often wondered where I would be if that person hadn't followed through- can you imagine? That is why following through with our feelings and promptings is so important! Because of this act of kindness, I immediately fell in love with the art of giving! It felt so good! With my next paycheck, my son and I went to a nearby Krshna Temple where we had made friends with the monks and the cook there. They had graciously fed us over the years for free and I was ready to practice more of my limitlessness by donating what I could to their organization. It felt so good to give back and I could feel so much love and understanding from the guru of the temple as I happily put money in his donation box. By taking the first step, I was able to continue taking steps beyond my own limitations and into a world that held more possibilities for me. I realized that I wanted money not just to survive, but to be able to give to others. This drove me to make different decisions about my career and education. I began to feel empowered, and I began to climb my own staircase, one step at a time to create a life where I could exercise my new sense of empowerment through giving.

Archangel Uriel's Message To The Modern World: *"It is a very sacred thing to be given an idea. Ideas aren't meant to be mulled around, sat upon, and then talked out of. The mere fact that you have an idea to do anything is an indication that something bigger than you is talking to you-especially if your idea continues to repeatedly come into your mind. Your ideas are precious and fertile ground for attaining what you pray for. In essence, many times your ideas are your answered prayers. The first step always appears after you have committed to the idea. However, you often do not see the first step because you are looking for the last one. You will see the last step when you get there. When you receive an idea, focus on finding the first step. As life unfolds for you with each step, you will find yourself in the magic. You will be in awe as your future is indeed created right in front of you by a perfect design and in the perfect direction. For there are rewards in each step, and each one is a celebration to be had."*

Questions To Consider: Are you paying attention to your ideas and thoughts? Do you trust your inner knowing when it comes to what steps to take? Can you reach into your inner nature and like a lightning bolt, blast through your fears and limitations to your desired destination? What do you need to prepare yourself for success? And finally, are you capable of moving forward like a storm regardless of the world around you and what people's reactions might be? These are things you will want to consider if you want to be the illuminated, powerful, and bright Archangel Uriel!

Chapter 15

Archangel Zadkiel- The Forgiver

Give Forth

The smell of burning sage and incense filled the air, along with beautiful music played by live instruments and drums. She had flowers in her hair, he wore his best shirt. They were surrounded by a large group of inviting people who had gathered together for a common purpose, and there was a sense of community and acceptance all around. She had hugged people she didn't know and he had let down his guard. When the ceremony began, everyone gathered around the fire hand in hand. Songs were sung, words were spoken, but they all knew why they had come. Under the full moon's light, one by one, each individual stepped forward and into the fire burned their fears, worries, doubts, and regrets. One by one, they were heard by the others, supported, and comforted. One by one, their burdens were turned to ashes, and one by one spirits were lifted. She finally mourned her losses; he finally came out of denial. And all was given forth that night with united intentions to forgive. "I am sorry, please forgive me, I love you, thank you." Hearts were mended; consciences were cleared, a new way opened to them. "And so it is."

I can't imagine a better Archangel to discuss in the final chapter of this book than Archangel Zadkiel. That is because his assignment and purpose really encompasses the foundation for healing for me. He is the Archangel of compassion and forgiveness. Compassion and forgiveness are developed through trials and lessons, and if you've ever wondered what your life purposes are, two of them might very well be to learn these virtues. We have danced around compassion and forgiveness throughout this book, however in the energy of Archangel Zadkiel, it is time to get very real and focus on what exactly is required of us to know and become one with their essence.

If Archangel Zadkiel were human, he would most likely be a guru or saint who willingly chose to live his life serving humanity. He would write books and have many followers. He would live very simply, wear simple yet useful clothing and living in an ashram or some sort of temple. He would travel the world and give speeches and talks that would radically change the minds and hearts of his listeners. He would be an eloquent speaker and a joy to interact with. I truly believe that if he were human, our world would be radically different. So many of our judgments, criticisms, prejudices, reasons for war, revenge, segregation, attacks, and self righteousness, stem from a perception of unforgiveness and lack of compassion. He would be a shining example and an easy man to follow.

Archangel Zadkiel's name means "Righteousness of God." I don't believe that in this context, righteousness means 'better than, or self righteous.' I believe it means truth and pure alignment to our creator. Archangel Zadkiel can help us work through the illusion of our pain and suffering and help us to find forgiveness and compassion for ourselves and others. He is an important Archangel. The inability to give forth our perceptions is ultimately where our pain and suffering come from. He works tirelessly to unveil our sight so that we can see the truth.

Archangel Zadkiel would probably practice yoga, read spiritual texts, go on nature walks, tend to animals, and serve many humanitarian causes. He would be very attractive, not only in looks, but his eyes would hold a special twinkle of youth and innocence. He would have a very grand sense of humor, and jokes would be common. You'd typically find him building schools and collecting books for undeveloped countries, assisting various charities and causes, speaking at United Nations Counsel about world peace, and actively helping us let go of our grievances and learn forgiveness and compassion. At the end of the day, he would feel peace and a deep sense of joy and happiness. His circle of friends would be close, uplifting, and supportive. You would find him in deep meditation before bed, and he would sleep deeply knowing that in truth, all is well in his world.

When I was first taught the idea of forgiveness, I understood it like this: Whenever someone hurts you, you have to forgive them because that is the Christian way of doing things. Christ forgave everyone, and so who are you to hold a grudge? If you don't forgive someone, you'll go to hell, so be the bigger person and take the high road and forgive them for what they have done to you. Or else.

I don't know how the process of forgiveness was explained to you, but over the years of assisting people through their painful past, this seems to be a common definition. On those pretenses, many of us go through the motions of forgiveness lest we burn and be punished for being an unforgiving person. But deep down inside there is still hate, anger, and a festering grudge infecting our hearts and minds creating havoc in our relationships and disrupting our happiness. Taking an authentic look at how we are still holding onto the pain of what someone has done to us takes a lot of self self-honesty, and no one likes to admit they have buried their unresolved feelings, because not only does it bring the pain up again, but you'll judge yourself for hanging on. Besides that, many of us believe that by forgiving someone, we are letting them off the hook for what they have done. We are afraid that if we let go of the pain and move on we will somehow be condoning their actions. Meanwhile, it is in our wounded nature to want to punish people to the extent that they hurt us. We yearn to lash back, to do unto them what they have done to us. It seems unfair that anyone would be able to get away with harmful actions, and our inner judge and jury find them guilty and punishable. We say things like, "justice will prevail, just wait until they meet their Maker." We wish God's wrath upon them because we feel helpless and small.

My own personal epiphany regarding forgiveness came while reading "A Course in Miracles." Until I read the following definition given in that book, I had assumed I knew what forgiveness was. Understanding what I read was both powerful and painful, as a very large part of me did not want to believe. I offer it here for you to mull over. Take your time with the following words, and really let them sink in. You may even want to read each small paragraph more than once. Pay attention to the part of you that resists what it's saying, and ask yourself why you would disagree or fight against this possible new belief.

For clarity purposes, when "A Course in Miracles" mentions, "God's Son," it is referring to you, me, and all of us. The word "sin" means that an error of thinking has taken place and a "miracle" is a correction in thinking to align to the truth that you are not separate from God.

"Forgiveness recognizes what you thought your brother did to you has not occurred. It does not pardon sins and make them real. It sees there was no sin. And in that view are all your sins forgiven. What is sin, except a false idea about God's Son? Forgiveness merely sees its falsity, and therefore lets it go. What then is free to take its place is now the Will of God.

An unforgiving thought is one which makes a judgment that it will not raise to doubt, although it is not true. The mind is closed, and will not be released. The thought protects projection, tightening its chains, so that distortions are more veiled and more obscure; less easily accessible to doubt, and further kept from reason. What can come between a fixed projection and the aim that it has chosen as its wanted goal?

An unforgiving thought does many things. In frantic action it pursues its goal, twisting and overturning what it sees as interfering with its chosen path. Distortion is its purpose, and the means by which it would accomplish it as well. It sets about its furious attempts to smash reality, without concern for anything that would appear to pose a contradiction to its point of view.

Forgiveness, on the other hand, is still, and quietly does nothing. It offends no aspect of reality, nor seeks to twist it to appearances it likes. It merely looks, and waits, and judges not. He who would not forgive must judge, for he must justify his failure to forgive. But he who would forgive himself must learn to welcome truth exactly as it is.

Do nothing, then, and let forgiveness show you what to do, through Him Who is your Guide, your Savior and Protector, strong in hope, and certain of your ultimate success. He has forgiven you already, for such is His function, given Him by God. Now must you share His function, and forgive whom He has saved, whose sinlessness He sees, and whom He honors as the Son of God."

For me, accepting that there was nothing to forgive was the hardest. Remember the story I told you about The Little Soul and The Sun in Archangel Raguels section? I had to remember that no one was created to be evil. We were all made in the likeness and image of our Creator, and therefore in truth, we are all perfect. However, we all wanted this human experience and this required us to be deeply hurt and betrayed by people. I thought I had forgiven those who had hurt me until I chose to see who they were beyond their actions, and beyond the role they had to play in my life. When I understood the entire picture, and was able to see their light beneath their mask- even when they could no longer see it themselves- I was set free.

So you see, forgiveness isn't just being the bigger person. It's seeing that they are too. Honestly, that's the hard part. No one wants to see the light within the person who's done their worst. But to me, that is our part of the contract. When the little soul in the sun thanks his friend for putting on the cloak and promises to remember them when they do their worst... THAT is forgiveness. You are essentially giving forth the illusion, seeing the truth behind every mask and false impression, and realizing that there is nothing to forgive and everything to learn.

At my weakest moments of wrestling with grievances I have cried out, "I want God more than I want this!" Recognizing that any hurt or grudge I have harbored in my heart can actually interfere with my ability to hear God clearly in my life has made it easier to let things go. Think about something you're struggling with and ask yourself what you want more- To feel God's love, or that? When put in that perspective, perhaps your prayer then becomes a very honest conversation about how deep down inside what you really want is to feel LOVED and that you may need help uncovering the grievances that interfere with your ability to feel it.

Compassion is the result of forgiveness. It is the natural softening that takes place when our understanding is expanded and we see the entire situation from a bird's eye view. Our walls are taken down; our defenses are now useless because there is nothing to defend ourselves against anymore. When we are able to see our enemies' light, it is then easy to see the light in everyone. It is easy to see it within ourselves.

And what about the times you have had to play the bad guy? That's right; you're not here to just be a victim that gets to overcome everyone else's wrongdoings. There will be a time in your life when it hits you that you are the one who requires forgiveness. It sucks, trust me. Realizing that I've played the role of the bad guy in certain situations and relationships has been way worse than being the recipient of hurt. Learning how to let myself off of the hook and practicing what "A Course in Miracles" teaches has been what has set me free in those times, and reminds me that through any seeming mistake, I'm still perfect at my core. Anytime we practice true forgiveness towards ourselves, we develop compassion towards ourselves. We become kind and easy with others because there are no grudges anywhere inside of us.

Now, I'm not saying this is easy. In fact, practicing these things is hard as hell. It takes daily work, prayer, humility, strength, and a deep willingness to trust and let things go when our minds want to hang on so badly. It is not easy, however it is attainable, it is possible, and it is extremely effective.

Another resource for learning about forgiveness came to me from the much beloved Louise L. Hay. Louise is like the fairy godmother I dreamed of having as a child. Although she didn't appear to dress me in a gown and send me to the ball, she instead helped to mend my broken heart and send me into the world again sparkling like a princess. The following are her words and serve as a salve to the inner wounds caused by unforgiveness. You can find the quotes below in her book, "You Can Heal Your Life," and on her Hay House blog.

"When you blame another, you give your own power away because you're placing the responsibility for your feelings on someone else. People in your life may behave in ways that trigger uncomfortable responses in you. However, they didn't get into your mind and create the buttons that have been pushed. Taking responsibility for your own feelings and reactions is mastering your 'ability to respond.' In other words, you learn to consciously choose rather than simply react.

Learning how to forgive yourself and others is a tricky and confusing concept for many people, but know that there's a difference between forgiveness and acceptance. Forgiving someone doesn't mean that you condone their behavior! The act of forgiveness takes place in your own mind. It really has nothing to do with the other person. The reality of true forgiveness lies in setting yourself free from the pain. It's simply an act of releasing yourself from the negative energy that you've chosen to hold on to. Also, forgiving yourself or others for past mistakes doesn't mean allowing the painful behaviors or actions of another to continue in your life. Sometimes forgiveness means letting go: You forgive that person and then you release them. Taking a stand and setting healthy boundaries is often the most loving thing you can do—not only for yourself, but for the other person as well.

No matter what your reasons are for having bitter, unforgiving feelings, you can go beyond them. You have a choice. You can choose to stay stuck and resentful, or you can do yourself a favor by willingly forgiving what happened in the past; letting it go; and then moving on to create a joyous, fulfilling life. You have the freedom to make your life anything you want it to be because you have freedom of choice."

How You Can Be Like Archangel Zadkiel

You must learn how to forgive yourself: true forgiveness where you are willing to see yourself as the person who is made in the likeness and image of your creator. See yourself as radiant, perfect, healed, whole, and complete for this is truly who you are past all of your judgments, misperceptions, and lack of self acceptance and self compassion. And while you're at it, rid your mind of other people's judgments of you; give forth any and all titles and names that were given to you by others that don't fit. See yourself as an innocent child who deserves love, care, and kindness. Then you will be able to direct this healing into all areas of your life. When you let yourself off the hook, you will be able to let others off the hook.

"Forgiveness is the fragrance that the violet sheds on the heel that has crushed it."-Mark Twain

The Mind State

Witnessing: Just seeing acts of kindness and forgiveness affects the witness. Be a witness. Look for it. Kindness is not typically posted everywhere, it isn't covered in the news, and you rarely see it on TV, social media, or movies. (Although, I would love to change that!) However, if you look around, you will see it everywhere. Witnessing kindness and forgiveness raises your serotonin levels (happy hormones) and instills core feelings of safety and security. When you become a witness to the goodness of life, it becomes a part of who you are.

Humility: Self-righteousness is learned behavior. Someone at some point judged you, and taught you wrongly that there is a hierarchy among humans. Because the feeling of being judged was so real and painful, you bought into the idea that there was a chance of being less-than enough. Then, in order to make yourself feel better, you had to find someone to judge and throw down beneath you. This is a very deep seated reality that probably started with our ancestors who were concerned with survival. The better humans survived, and the ones at the bottom of the totem pole did not. Archangel Zadkiel is here to say that we don't have to live like that anymore. We have evolved past the need to judge the fittest for survival, and that is why it no longer feels right.

People who judge others have a big problem with judging themselves. Insecurity, low confidence, and feeling unworthy are all issues that fuel the need to judge others. Also, if someone has been raised with super 'judgy' parents or siblings, they may grow up to be very critical of others as they will likely have been raised feeling overly criticized themselves, and are now filled with self-criticism.

Remember, there really isn't anything to forgive in the truth that we are all equally God's creation. We are all just players acting out roles in our lives so that we can learn, grow, and become better. This helps us to be humble and stay out of self righteousness. Be willing to stay open and aware of what treasures others can bless you with, knowing that no one is beneath you or above you. Your ego will hate this idea because it thrives on hierarchy. If there is any piece of you that resists equality, I suggest working on that mind state until it is healed.

Compassion: When you are open to forgive yourself and everyone around you, your heart softens and your world becomes beautiful. Your heaviness falls away, you begin to glow with an undeniable radiance. Life becomes easier because you are less burdened by the past, and the decisions you make from a compassionate heart will always lead you to happiness. When you are willing to give people the benefit of the doubt, or understand where they are coming from, you are showing mercy. This is easy to do when you can recognize the Divine in every creature. It is easy to love and accept others as you learn how to love and accept yourself. This is the truth of the open and compassionate heart.

The Work

Who are you judging right now? Who are you picking apart and/or criticizing? Be honest; you *are* being self righteous in some way. Everyone has something that makes them feel justified in judging another person, so dig deep- you'll find it. Watch yourself, and some sort of ugly inner judge will emerge from within you at some point. It's time to look really deep and ask yourself what benefit you are getting by riding your high horse. What is it about you that needs to criticize another? Or in other words, what part of your own self-judgment is being triggered by the actions of another person?

And now turning these questions around, who is working right now to forgive you? Is there anything you can do to help them understand forgiveness for what it is? And how can you practice forgiveness towards yourself?

You can use my all time favorite forgiveness affirmations anytime you feel yourself spiraling into the illusion:

- "I forgive the part of me that judges the part of you from my unhealed perception."
- "I now take my power back from this situation and let go of anything that does not serve my forward movement."
- "I am capable of moving beyond my mistakes."
- "I relax and let this go."
- "I accept that I did the best that I could at the time with what I knew."
- "As I let others off the hook, I let myself off the hook, and we are all free."
- "I take from this situation all of the lessons and wisdom, and release all pain and suffering."
- "I chose to see God's light within me, the other person, and this entire situation now, trusting that as I move beyond my limiting perceptions, that all is truly well and in order."

Commit to sharing, posting, or discussing some sort of act of kindness every single day. Can you imagine how different the world would be if we all chose to engage in positive interactions instead of spreading drama and the ill-effects of judgment and unforgiveness? If every single person who reads this book just did that one thing... just imagine the difference!

Real Life

One of the most compelling stories of forgiveness I have ever had the honor of witnessing comes from a close friend of mine. She has graciously allowed me to share this story and I am forever grateful to her for that because I know it will touch many hearts. For the sake of her family's privacy, I changed her name to Grace- since that is ultimately what she is an example of.

When Grace was 8 her father was violently murdered. Her father was a chef, and had decided to go into work early one morning only to happen upon a coworker robbing the store's safe. When the robber saw her father, he stabbed him multiple times and left him there to suffer and die. I cannot imagine how my friend, at such an innocent age handled the news of her father being violently murdered.

Through the years, Grace found herself hating the man who murdered her father. So many countless times she wanted her father, and he couldn't be there because of this man. Every time there was an event in her life, or activities at school that required her father, she was reminded of a life that was taken from her. So many times she wondered how her father's presence would have influenced her life. And each time she missed him, cried for him, needed him, and begged God to bring him back, her heart was hardened towards the man who had taken him away from her.

As justified as her anger was, it placed her inside of a cold, hard prison of her own making. She grew up not trusting people, and being closed to love and success. She found herself feeling jealous of all of the other girls who grew up with fathers, and she developed a very strong attachment to being a victim. This victim mentality grew into every area of her life and she found herself struggling, failing, losing, and spiraling down into a pattern where nothing ever worked out for her. She says that life was just very hard growing up. Her mother struggled; everyone always seemed to struggle, so this became her norm as she grew into a young woman.

Grace knew she needed help and sought out healing from gentle Reiki practitioners, energy healers, and books like "The Little Soul and The Sun." She found peace and healing within the self help and new age community, and over time she realized that by not forgiving her father's murderer, she was only allowing the pain to continue. She knew that while her father's life was taken from him, she had to begin to live her own. Living in the pain of unforgiveness was no life to live. This required her to accept what had happened and begin the steps toward healing herself and as she did, her victim mentality was replaced by a strong force of light that carries her through to this day.

Grace had the opportunity to face her father's murderer at his parole hearing years after she healed her heart. She had worked on herself, her mind state, and had become a very strong young woman by then.

As Grace sat in the courtroom, her family and other witnesses all focused on her, she read out loud the letter that would change everything. No, she couldn't bring her father back. But, Grace deserved freedom from her own prison. She was finally ready to forgive and set herself free.

These are small excerpts of the letter she read to her father's killer at a parole hearing. Although her family is mentioned throughout original letter, I have chosen to leave out her family's experiences- including their names and the name of the murderer- for the sake of privacy, and to focus on the forgiveness that was offered:

" My name is 'Grace', I am the oldest daughter. (States siblings and mother's name) My family was affected by (name of murderer), never to be the same again. Our father has been missing from our lives since we were very young. My mom was deeply affected and has never remarried or even been on a date. She has raised us on her own staying true to the only man she ever loved. She may not admit this, but deep down she is lonely and depressed. She has had no partner to talk to, cry with, laugh with, and love. However, she is a strong woman who has taught us strength of nobility.

...I am now 28. Age of scarring 8 yrs. old. 8- the age when I had to grow up and become an adult. I had to help take care of not only my brothers and sister but my mom. I had to make sure that my mom was eating, that she got up to take care of us and that she felt loved so that we didn't lose her also. I was a little girl with a world of responsibility. That same year in December, my grandma, (mom's mother) passed away. All I could do was tell my mom that we now had 2 angels watching over us and that my Papi

now had someone to take care of him too. I have nightmares that have stayed with me my entire life, horrible dreams that are so real that I still to this day have to convince myself that they exist only in another world; that my reality is far different than the terror that paralyzes me from the depths of my fears. I have lived my ups and downs, life has been so hard. However, I do want to say that I forgive you. I don't know what it is like to have a father figure in my life but because of the experiences that I have had to deal with I am a much stronger daughter, woman, and mother. I am ambitious, I am hard working, and I am trying to live up to the man my father was.

...I may be a better woman because (I have healed myself from) your actions, but I never want to walk the same streets with you....I ask the parole board to take in consideration that (murderer) exchanged the death sentence for life in prison, and it is the wish of my family that he serves his sentence of life in prison without parole. Thank you for your time and consideration."

I was not there, however I imagine there was not one dry eye in the courtroom. This included the prisoner, of whom my friend tells me had begun sobbing loudly and remorsefully. When the court allowed him a reply it was simply, "You have done something for me I have not been able to do for myself." Words that will forever fill Grace's mind as she moves on and into her freedom. Her father's killer was given a life sentence without parole, however many doors were opened that day. Her forgiveness allowed others to finally accept what had happened, and begin their own healing. Her forgiveness allowed the murderer the opportunity to be touched by grace before he was put to a life sentence. But most of all, her forgiveness opened the door to her heart so that she could finally feel her father's presence. In spirit, he had been there with her all along, however her anger had shut off any feeling from the other side. She began to build her life, one that included love, softness, and peace.

Of course, this is only one of countless stories where forgiveness and redemption prevails. I am sure you personally know of someone who showed extreme faith, courage, and mercy in the face of the worst happening to them. These stories are important to keep in the forefront of our minds in the midst of so many petty grudges and resentments that we so justifiably cling to.

We see the ugliness with people who try to punish others with anger and hurt thinking it is their right to do so. Think of all of the ugly divorces that trap children in a prison of hate and heartbreak. Think of the shallow gossip, the lies, backstabbing, deceit, and blatant revenge that comes from the unforgiving heart. Now think of my friend Grace.

So your ex is a cheat, so your parent is a low life, so your family judges you, so your boss is a liar, so your best friend betrayed you. I know, I know, I know- trust me, I know. As someone who has been through a lot of hurt too, I know. You think you have every right to your behavior. But here's the truth: If you are really ready to live your life the way it was meant to be lived, if you really want to be the badass you are, and if you really want to save yourself and join the team of powerful Archangels, you'll assume the right to remember who you are, remember who the bad guys are, and forgive what has been done. Stop the cycles.

Look at the many victims of your hardened heart. It isn't just the person you hate, it's everyone who wishes to be loved by you but can't because you're so busy trying to punish one person. For the rest of her life, Grace will always be able to say to anyone who hurts her, "I forgave the person who did his worst to me and my family. I can forgive this." Come onto the path of forgiveness! Once you forgive the worst, it becomes easy- it becomes your norm. Take accountability for your part, release yourself from the chains and the heaviness that you yourself have created and open your own prison door. Life is not easier with justifications. Life is easier when you finally give them up, and liberate yourself! Countless blessings and goodness are waiting for your opened and softened heart.

Archangel Zadkiel's Message To The Modern World: *"If there was one thing I wish every single one of you would understand deeply it is this: YOU. ARE. DESERVING. You deserve love. You deserve kindness. You deserve happiness. You deserve compassion to dwell in your holy heart. You deserve to feel connected to your Creator, and to have Divine experiences. You deserve to have your needs met. You deserve to have your dreams and desires fulfilled. You deserve to be free from addiction. You deserve to live. You deserve to see yourself through the eyes of us angels, and you deserve to perceive yourself as your Creator sees you. This is His will for you. Don't you see? We Angels and the entire universe are constantly conspiring for your highest good. We live to see even a simple* *smile across your face. There is so much that goes on behind the scenes to help you along this journey. Let us help. You deserve this help. Open up and allow the good to rush in knowing that YOU. ARE. DESERVING."*

Questions To Consider: How can you be the example of compassion and forgiveness to others? What steps do you need to take right now to begin to see yourself as perfect, whole, healed, and complete- even when the illusion tells you otherwise? These are things you will have to consider if you want to be like the forgiving, compassionate, joyful, peaceful, healer Archangel Zadkiel.

Conclusion

Joining the 15 means that you are willing to set aside your grievances and negativity in exchange for stepping into your powerful magnificence. It also means that you understand that nothing outside of yourself can give you peace, and that nobody else has the power to save you. But this also means that nothing outside yourself can truly hurt you, disturb your peace, or upset you in any way. Understanding this idea places you in charge of your life where you belong, because of who you are and Who's you are. Joining the 15 means that you are ready to trust in your Creator, and know that He would never place a remedy or answer for your unhappiness, illness, or fear where you couldn't find it. God and the angels want you to be healed, happy, whole, prosperous, and complete.

Are you ready to stop looking in external places for love, peace, and joy? Are you ready to fall in love with yourself and with your life, and rise to the challenges you stand against so that you can learn who you really are and what you're really about? Are you ready to be the angel to others that your angels have been for you? Are you ready to live the life you were born to- the one your Creator wants for you? If so, then declare it. Scream it from the mountain tops! Heaven needs your undivided and unmistakable resounding "YES!!!"

As you join forces with Heaven, it will become apparent to you and to the world. Through your example, you will remind everyone of their own potential and magnificence! As "A Course in Miracles" affirms, "My salvation comes from me. Nothing outside of me can hold me back. Within me is the world's salvation and my own." You truly are the light within the dark!

I now wish to give you some well deserved recognition for everything you've been through to get you to this point. Because here is the reality that we all face: When you put this book down and go out into your life, you will inevitably be faced with challenges. Life can come at you fast and furious like a bull charging for the kill. I've been there- in the midst of something stressful completely forgetting who I am and who walks by my side. I have been terrified of being hurt, wounded, and lost.

This world, as it has been explained to me, is one of the most difficult places in the entire universe to exist in. Wars, famine, heartache, disease, and so much drama! The very fact that you are here in this arena with me tells me you are a badass. The very fact that your soul incarnated on this planet tells me that you are a veteran. As I look around at the homeless, the addicts, the hurt, the overworked and underappreciated, I see you. You are all warriors in my eyes. You get tired and fed up, you feel the pain of this world, and sometimes you feel insignificant and gone astray. I get it. The fact that anyone got up this morning is remarkable if you think about it. And if you got up with a smile on your face, ready to take on another incredible day on this planet then my hat goes off to you!

Whenever I feel like giving up, these thoughts remind me how to get back up and keep going: *I am the light I've been searching for in the dark. I am never alone.* We are in this together. We are soldiers, fighting our own battles and leveling up one victory at a time.

I want to tell you that you may find yourself flat on the ground at times, and it's okay. We all take a turn falling down and forgetting who we really are. What I'm here to do is to remind you! You have an entire team of fellow soldiers and 15 powerful Archangels here to help you up again and remind you of the truth. You really are your own angel- you are the one you've been waiting for, and no matter where you have journeyed, whatever mess you find yourself in, you have had the power to save yourself every...single...time! Whatever you are going through right now in your life, you can now be just like the angels! We can collectively be angels for each other and do what they would do!

Never.

Give.

Up.

With our world changing and evolving at this rapid speed, we can't lie down. We must come together with ourselves, with each other, and with Heaven to create peace on earth- which is what we all want.

Welcome to the team!

"Take a stand." -Archangel Ariel

"Remember that love never dies." -Archangel Azrael

"What you are looking for is not out there."- Archangel Chamuel

"Say what you need to say." -Archangel Gabriel

"Your love changes things." -Archangel Haniel

"Mistakes are proof you're trying. It's okay to make them." -Archangel Jeremiel

"Put your best self out there." -Archangel Jophiel

"Wake up, kick ass, repeat." -Archangel Metatron

"Be brave." -Archangel Michael

"Everything happens for a reason." -Archangel Raguel

"Heal thyself." -Archangel Rapheal

"Some things are not meant to be understood, but accepted." -Archangel Raziel

"Chill." Archangel Sandalphon

"The best way to predict the future is to create it." -Archangel Uriel

"Forgive." -Archangel Zadkiel

"You've got this! Now chin up, shoulders back, spread your wings and FLY!" -Crystal Dawn Doty

FAQ'S

What if I don't believe in angels?

You don't have to believe in angels in order to get great information on how to better your life. They can be more like subjects, archetypes, and personas. As far as I know, angels don't really care of you believe in them or not. Their job is not to prove their existence, and that isn't my intention either. Their job is to make the world a better place. We can all learn from that idea; that if we focus on improving ourselves and making the world around us better, it becomes less about "ME" and more about "WE." You don't have to believe in angels in order to act like one.

I notice that you talk about the Archangels as if they are male or female, what's up with angels having genders?

Angels aren't human and so they don't have sex organs. However, male and female energy doesn't require or depend on organs. Their personalities and purpose categorize them into a more male or female persona. Archangel Gabriel is probably the most controversial, as she's depicted as male in the bible but yet many people who intuitively see and interact with her see her as more female. Plus, she's associated with pregnancy and babies and that is commonly more of a female thing.

If you think about what Archangel Michael represents, his purpose and calling, you would definitely classify him as male energy whereas Archangel Haniel is extremely feminine. Again, it's not that they have genders as much as what they represent has a male or female essence.

You suggest getting rid of the word "should." What are we supposed to replace the word "should" with?

You can replace it with the words "deserve" and "get to." Example: Instead of saying that your kids should clean their rooms, they get to clean their rooms; they deserve to have clean rooms. Instead of saying, I should be doing more, say I get to do more, I deserve to feel better than this.

Could angels really be aliens?

Angels can be whatever you want them to be. You can believe they are aliens, ascended masters, orbs of light, gifts from God, aliens, Bigfoot, or simply examples and role models who help you become a better person.

What if I want to connect more to the angels?

I offer a mentorship and one on one coaching to help you open and exercise your intuitive abilities and connection to your angels. Please check my website for details. www.clarityistheway.com

Do we pray to angels? What if God gets mad that we are discussing them and not him?

I personally do not pray to angels, I pray to God. I talk to the angels like I am talking to you, or to a friend. I go to them for help, comfort, and insight just as I would a counselor, mentor, or teacher. I don't believe God gets angry with us. I believe that anger and jealousy are human emotions that are often and unfortunately projected onto God. God is THE source of Love and to me He remains steady and unwavering in His Love for us. He doesn't have the egotistical need to be discussed or even worshipped. That's all for our benefit, not His. I do know that He wants us to be happy. His angels are gifts for us to use, and He joyfully gives us permission to use all of His gifts for our happiness.

Did you listen to any particular music while writing this book?

I mostly had new age and classical music softly playing in the background. I have a hard time writing to songs that have words because it makes me want to dance around and sing along instead of write. I did get into a weird funk and experienced a bit of writer's block just before I began writing Archangel Michael's section. I realized that my surroundings were too soft for what I wanted to be writing so I rocked out to music that helped me feel tough and like a warrior. Once in awhile I have to stop writing, take a break and goof off to my favorite music to keep the juices flowing.

Was there anything that was particularly hard for you to write?

Archangel Azrael always brings a tear to my eye because he has been there so much for me and my family during times of grief and transition.

193

There were many times my heart felt full of love, gratitude, and admiration for each Archangel I was writing about and I would have to grab some tissues.

I also have family and friends who believe very different things than I do, and I worried about offending them. But I knew that certain things just had to be said, for the sake of this book and the sake of everyone who is willing to do what angels would do. Putting myself out there is pretty scary, but at the end of the day I can't be holding back for the sake of offending people. I'd rather be authentic and proud of my book, rather than pleasing everyone and disappointing myself.

What helped you to stay focused while writing?

I joined a couple mastermind mentoring groups, hearing other entrepreneurs go after their dreams and work hard really motivates me. I also followed my favorite published authors on various social medias. Seeing their success and watching how awesome their lives are really keeps me focused on achieving my own personal goals. Talking to other authors and learning from my friend, Niki Livingston, who has self published a fiction/fantasy series helped me a lot. Most of all, it's easy for me to stay focused when I'm surrounded by so much support and friends who understand and honor why I am crazy busy. My followers have been so excited about this book and knowing there were people who were exciting and waiting kept me focused on finishing it.

Other ways I stay focused: I love ballet, playing piano, painting, and reading. Engaging in those things on a regular basis keeps my creativity flowing. On the days I feel unmotivated, I will put on some cute leg warmers and practice ballet warm up routines. Dancing reminds me that I am elegant, graceful, and flexible. I also love being out in nature, and so just a simple walk to the park can give me the breath of fresh air to stay rejuvenated. By taking time out away from my writing, I'm able to restart and then when I sit back down to write and I am flooded with inspiration. And then there's coffee...

How do I recommend this book to others?

The best advice in this area is to do what Archangel Michael says, and be the change first. Use the information in this book to propel your life forward. Once you make changes, and you start to act, look and feel better, people will ask you what your secret is. Then you can say something like this: "You know that thing I've always wanted to do, or that goal I've always wanted to accomplish? Well, I read something that really helped me discover how to do it." Unsolicited recommendations rarely work. You know what this book is all about, and you know that by utilizing it how powerful it is. Share it wisely.

Acknowledgements

I want to thank Zoe Freeman for her hard work with editing this material. Zoe, you really pushed me to write more, to be crystal clear, and I know the angels appreciated how you softened a lot my edginess. Thank you for sticking it out with me, and for helping me birth my dream. Your support is priceless.

Thank you to my big brother from another mother, Warren Merrill for stepping in and helping me to step it up! You are a true example of what an Archangel would do in human form. Thank you for your attention to detail and for your honesty. This book has been blessed by you!!!

Thank you to my son, Nathaniel Doty, who also contributed a lot to the editing process. Thank you for being the "coma police,,,," I love you! Thank you to my sweet little Nicholas Anderson, who also helped by being patient with me and writing sweet little love notes of encouragement on my whiteboard along the way. He was so excited when I told him that his mommy was going to write a book about angels, and his enthusiasm means so much! Nick, you are my light!

Thank you to Niki Livingston, my BFF and fellow author. Your experience and knowledge from publishing before me has been gold. Your support and love is so amazing- from the time we were teenagers until we are old ladies. Cheers to our timeless friendship.

Doreen Virtue has to be acknowledged here because if it wasn't for her years of dedication and work regarding the angels, I would not be writing this today. When I grow up, I hope to be half the woman she is. Doreen, "thank you" will never be enough to say for what you have shown me and everyone who follows you. Aloha and Namaste.

Finally, to Father God and Mother Goddess, Jesus, all of my angels, guides and fae- You are my family. You have always been here for me, and now it's my turn to be here for you! May your light be the beacon that illuminates every single heart and may your love reign supreme in this world forever. I love you, I love you, I love you, Amen.

Made in the USA
Monee, IL
31 January 2020